Competition Law in Peru

Competition Law in Peru

Second Edition

Alfredo Bullard González
Agustín Valencia-Dongo

This book was originally published as a monograph in the International Encyclopaedia of Laws/Competition Law.

Founding Editor: Roger Blanpain
General Editor: Frank Hendrickx
Volume Editors: Francesco Denozza & Alberto Toffoletto

Wolters Kluwer

Published by:
Kluwer Law International B.V.
PO Box 316
2400 AH Alphen aan den Rijn
The Netherlands
E-mail: lrs-sales@wolterskluwer.com
Website: www.wolterskluwer.com/en/solutions/kluwerlawinternational

Sold and distributed by:
Wolters Kluwer Legal & Regulatory U.S.
7201 McKinney Circle
Frederick, MD 21704
United States of America
E-mail: customer.service@wolterskluwer.com

ISBN 978-94-035-4390-1

e-Book: ISBN 978-94-035-4400-7
web-PDF: ISBN 978-94-035-4410-6

The Authors

Alfredo Bullard is a partner at Bullard, Falla, Ezcurra +, a firm that has gained experience over the past sixteen years advising and representing highest-profile companies in Peru in proceedings before Peruvian Competition Authority. Alfredo was born in 1964 and holds his degree in Law from Pontificia Universidad Católica del Perú (PUCP) and his master's (LLM) from the University of Yale, U.S.A. He is a former President of the Tribunal for the Defense of Competition and Protection of Intellectual Property of INDECOPI (National Institute for the Defense of Competition and Protection of Intellectual Property). Alfredo has also been a Professor of Civil Law, Arbitration, Litigation and Economic Analysis of Law at Pontificia Universidad Católica del Perú.

Agustín Valencia-Dongo is a senior associate at Bullard, Falla, Ezcurra +, a firm that has gained experience over the past sixteen years advising and representing highest-profile companies in Peru in proceedings before Peruvian Competition Authority. Agustín was born in 1986 and holds his degree in Law from Pontificia Universidad Católica del Perú (PUCP) and his master's (MPP) from the University of Cambridge, U.K. Agustín has taught Competition Law, Unfair Competition Law and Consumer Protection Law at Universidad del Pacífico. He currently teaches Unfair Competition and Advertising Law as part of the Intellectual Property and Competition Law Master's program at Pontificia Universidad Católica del Perú.

The Authors' Assistants

The authors received invaluable assistance from the Bullard Falla Ezcurra + Competition team, particularly from Andrea Cadenas, Adriana Garcés, Romina Calonge and Lucía Cuglievan.

The Authors

Table of Contents

Table of Contents

List of Abbreviations

ADSL	Asymmetric Digital Subscriber List
CAN	Andean Community of Nations
CFC	Brewers Committee of the National Industries Society
COES	Economic Operation Committee of the National Grid
CSAV	Compañía Sudamericana de Vapores S.A.
DICAPI	Peruvian General Direction of Captaincy and Coastguards
FNE	*Fiscalía Nacional Económica*
FONAFE	*Fondo Nacional de Financiamiento de la Actividad Empresarial del Estado*
GDP	Gross Domestic Product
HHI	Herfindahl-Hirschman Index
HMT	Hypothetical Monopolist Test
INDECOPI	National Institute for the Defense of Competition and Protection of Intellectual Property
LDI	Long-Distance International
LPG	Liquefied Petroleum Gas
LRCA	Law for the Repression of Anticompetitive Conducts
MOL	Mitsui O.S.K. Lines Ltd.
NDC	National Directorate for the Surveillance and Promotion of Competition

List of Abbreviations

NYK	Nippon Yusen Kabushiki Kaisha
OECD	Organisation for Economic Co-operation and Development
OEFA	Environmental Protection Agency
OSCE	State Contracting Supervisor Agency
OSIPTEL	Supervisory Agency of Private Investment in Telecommunications
PROINVERSION	Peruvian Agency for Promotion of Investments
SBS	Banking and Insurance Superintendency
SIC	Superintendencia de Industria y Comercio
SMV	Securities Market Regulator
SSNIP	Small but Significant Non-Transitory Increase in Price
UIT	Tax Unit
VNG	Vehicular Natural Gas

English	**Spanish**
National Institute for the Defense of Competition and Protection of Intellectual Property	*Instituto Nacional de Defensa de la Competencia y Protección de la Propiedad Intelectual*
National Directorate for the Surveillance and Promotion of Competition	*Dirección Nacional de Investigación y Promoción de la Competencia*
Supervisory Agency of Private Investment in Telecommunications	*Organismo Supervisor de la Inversión Privada en Telecomunicaciones*
Law for the Repression of Anticompetitive Conducts	*Ley de Represión de Conductas Anticompetitivas*
Organisation for Economic Co-operation and Development	*Organización para el Desarrollo y Cooperación Económica*
Tax Reference Unit	*Unidad Impositiva Tributaria*
Andean Community of Nations	*Comunidad Andina de Naciones*
Complaint	*Denuncia*
Investigation	*Investigación*
Merger	*Fusión*
Law/Act	*Ley*
Rule	*Reglamento*

Interim Measure/Precautionary Measure/Injunction	*MedidaCautelar*
Antitrust Commission	*Comisión de Defensa de la Libre Competencia*

List of Abbreviations

General Introduction

§1. Peru: A General Background

I. Geography and Climate

1. Peru is located in the middle of the South American Pacific Zone and is the third-largest country in the region. With an extension of 1,285,216 km^2 and three geographical regions (coast, mountains and jungle), Peru has an extended and mega-diverse territory. Bordered by Ecuador and Colombia to the north, Brazil and Bolivia to the east, and Chile to the south, Peru is strategically located in South America, facing the vastest ocean in the world, the Pacific Ocean.

2. The combination of tropical latitude, mountain ranges, topography variations and two ocean currents (Humboldt and El Niño) gives Peru a large variety of climates and microclimates (twenty-eight of the thirty-two global climates). Commonly, three geographical zones are distinguished in order to describe Peru's diversity.

A. Coast

3. Near the Pacific Ocean, Peru has a subtropical climate with very little rainfall, which makes it common to find semiarid locations and deserts. In the Southern and the Central Coast regions rainfalls are uncommon (less than 100 mm per year). Temperature ranges from 8°C to 32°C, with warm moist summers and cool humid winters, determined by an almost permanent layer of fog. In the Northern coast region, Humboldt and El Niño Currents find each other, making both summer and winter hot, humid and sunny, with temperatures that range from 14°C to 38°C.

B. Mountain Region

4. Depending on the altitude, Peruvian Andes exhibit different temperatures and characteristics, which vary from 0°C to 32°C. From September to April, mountain region has a rainy season. The rest of the year has very hot and dry conditions during days, but cold nights.

C. Jungle

5. In the jungle, the summer or dry season, between April and October (ideal for tourism), is dominated by sunny days and high temperatures, often above 35°C. The moisture in the jungle is very high throughout the year. In the southern region there are occasional "friajes" or "surazos," cold fronts coming from the south of the continent that occur between the months of May and August, during which time the temperatures can drop to 8°C–12°C.

II. Population and Values

6. According to 2017 National Census,[1] the total population at that time was 31,237,385 people, with a population increase of 301,662 people per year. The dominant age range fluctuates between 15 and 64 years, which represent 65.2% of the population. In 2020, the middle age of the population was at 30.6 years. Twenty years ago it was 22.7 years, indicating that there are more elderly population.[2]

7. In Peru, there are sixty-four births and seventeen deaths per hour. Another item indicates that, at the national level, 249 marriages are registered every day, with ten every hour.[3]

8. The coast region concentrates 58% of the Peruvian population.[4] According to the results of the 2017 National Census, the five departments with the greatest percentage of population were: Lima with 32.3%, Piura with 6.3%, La Libertad with 6.1%, Arequipa with 4.7%, and Cajamarca with 4.6%. All together concentrate a little more than half of the total population (53.9%).

9. Lima, the capital of Peru, is considered the political, cultural, economic and commercial core of the country. Today it concentrates one-third of the total population. There is no doubt that the urbanization process in Peru is going really fast. One of the reasons started in 1940, when the relationship between man-land broke: rural population growth came to a point that the available land would not be enough hereinafter to sustain more habitants to be born. This triggered a crisis in the agricultural sector and led to the first great wave of migration. From this point, and over the following fifty years, the nature of the Peruvian society has changed radically. Cities became the main duty stations, especially Lima. Today, Lima continues to be the city that concentrates the largest proportion of the country's population.

1. This is the last official Census in Peru. INEI (2018). *Perú Resultados definitivos de los Censos Nacionales 2017*, Tomo I, Lima October 2018, https://bit.ly/3wynQXA (accessed Jun. 16, 2021).
2. INEI (2020). *Estado de la población peruana 2020.* Lima July 2020, https://bit.ly/2S1FYu9 (accessed Jun. 16, 2021).
3. INEI (2019). *Panorama demográfico.* Lima July 2019, https://bit.ly/3cOfNy5 (accessed Jun. 16, 2021).
4. CEPLAN (2019). *El Perú en el que vivimos: caracterización del territorio.* Lima January 2019, https://bit.ly/3vugXFG (accessed Jun. 16, 2021).

10. According to the World Bank data, Peru's life expectancy in 2019 was 77 years old.[5] At 80 years, women have a higher life expectancy[6] versus 74 years[7] for men. It is worth mentioning that there is a positive trend on the life expectancy in the country.

11. In connection with educational characteristics, according to the 2017 National Census, there has been an increase in the educational level in contrast to the previous National Census in 2007. One factor that explains this is that the population of Peruvians over fifteen years old with no educational level has decreased from 7.4% in 2007 to 5% in 2017. Likewise, illiteracy has been reduced by 1.3% in contrast to the previous National Census. In 2017, there were almost 1.3 million people aged 15 and over that were unable to read or write.

12. Since Peru used to be a Spanish colony, 82.6% percent of the population aged 5 and over speaks Spanish as their mother language. However, there are other languages that still remain from ancient cultures. As of the relevance of the other languages, 13.9% of the population considered Quechua as their mother language. It is followed by Aimara with 1.7% and other native languages with 0.5%.

13. The fact that Peru used to be a Spanish colony also explains why 17.6 million people profess the Catholic religion, which is equivalent to 81.3% of the registered population aged 12 and over, followed in importance by the population who profess the Evangelical religion, that reaches 14.1%, and other religions with 4.8% profess. Also, 5.1% of respondents said they have no religion.

14. By 2019, 64.5% of women of working age were participating in economic activities, which implies an increment of 1.2 percentage points compared with the results obtained in 2014.[8]

15. There are 2,703 indigenous communities located in eleven departments of the country. Indigenous populations are ancestrally settled on Peruvian Amazon, and they all belong to thirteen language "families." There is no other country in this continent with more language families than Peru.[9] The indigenous population of the Amazon is 212,823 habitants.[10]

---

5. http://datos.bancomundial.org/indicador/SP.DYN.LE00.IN/countries/PE?display=graph (accessed Jun. 16, 2021).
6. http://datos.bancomundial.org/indicador/SP.DYN.LE00.FE.IN/countries/PE?display=graph (accessed Jun. 16, 2021).
7. http://datos.bancomundial.org/indicador/SP.DYN.LE00.MA.IN/countries/PE?display=graph (accessed Jun. 16, 2021).
8. Economic activity rate of men and women, according to geographical area, https://bit.ly/2TFiP16 (accessed Jun. 16, 2021).
9. Dancé, J. (sf). *Los pueblos indígenas en la amazonía peruana: población y entorno ambiental*, https://bit.ly/2SyuIps (accessed Jun. 16, 2021).
10. INEI (2018). *Población Indígena u Originaria de la Amazonía*, https://bit.ly/3gHOBCg (accessed Jun. 16, 2021).

III. Government and Politics

16. Peru has had twelve constitutions throughout its republican history. The current Constitution from 1993 was approved during the government of Alberto Fujimori.

17. The regime is semi-presidential. The head of State is the head of government and is elected directly by the population every five years, being the vote mandatory and universal. The executive power is exercised fully by the government. The president has the power to appoint and dismiss ministers, who also require the confidence of Congress. The legislature may oppose such designations. It is important to mention that the President is able to dissolve the Congress, if it has censured or denied confidence of two councils of ministers.

18. The three branches of government (executive, legislative and judicial) are independent from each other. In addition, the Constitution created the Constitutional Tribunal as the autonomous control organ to guarantee the constitutionality of laws and actions of the organs of the State.

19. Legislative power has a single camera with 130 members. The congressmen are elected for terms of five years using the Multiple Constituency System. The seats are distributed proportionally to the number of voters in each constituency.

20. The party system is described as a "democracy without parties."[11] It is an atomized system of candidate-centered politics characterized by being fragmented and pragmatic. Despite this, we can identify three political parties with trajectory: the *Partido Aprista Peruano* (center-right)[12] since 1930, the *Partido Popular Cristiano* (center-right) since 1966 and *Acción Popular* (center-left) since 1956. Additionally, over the past three periods we can identify four relevant political parties: *PerúPosible* (center-right), *Solidaridad Nacional* (center-right), *Unión por el Perú* (center-left), and the *fujimorismo* (cent3r-right);[13] and over the past two periods: the *Partido Nacionalista Gana Perú* (center-left) and *Restauración Nacional* (center-right).[14]

11. Cameron A. Maxwell, Steven Levitsky. *Democracy Without Parties? Political Parties and Regime Change in Fujimori's Perú.* 55(3) Latin American Politics and Society 1–33 (2003). Miami: Centre for Latin American Studies at the University of Miami, https://bit.ly/35xnhBN (accessed Jun. 18, 2021).
12. The *Partido Aprista Peruano* began like a socialist political party. Then, their ideology moved to the center-right.
13. The *fujimorismo* changes its name each election. In the election of the 2011, the name of the inscription was *Fuerza 2011.*
14. Milagros Campos, *Congreso y Políticas Públicas,* Lima: Universidad del Pacífico, 2012, https://bit.ly/3gKOE0k (accessed Jun. 18, 2021).

§2. Economic System

I. Industries and Trade

21. Peru is an emerging, market-oriented economy characterized by a high level of foreign trade and foreign investment. Since the early 1990s, the country has implemented a series of macroeconomic reforms that, combined with a favorable external environment, have enabled an average gross domestic product (GDP) growth rate of 4.5% between 2010 and 2019.[15] This has resulted in an increase of more than 27% in Peru's per capita income during that same period, according to the Central Bank.[16]

22. It is relevant to mention that in 2020 public debt, as a share of GDP, was 34.8%. At the time, it was one of the lowest levels of debt in the region.[17] The main rating agencies, Standard & Poor's, Fitch, and Moody's qualified Peru as the second-lowest sovereign risk country within the region.[18]

23. Peru's economy reflects its varied geography. A wide range of important natural resources are found in the mountainous, Amazonian and coastal areas. Its main industries are mining and refining of minerals (copper, gold, lead, zinc and silver, among others); petroleum extraction and refining; natural gas and natural gas liquefaction; and fishing and fishing processing. Agriculture is also an important economic activity. The main crops include asparagus, coffee, cocoa, cotton, sugarcane, potatoes, corn and rice.

24. Exports have increased 33% over the last decade (2010–2019). In 2020, the volume of exports was USD 42.4 billion. Peru's main export products are minerals, crude petroleum, natural gas, fishmeal, coffee, asparagus, machinery and textiles. By 2020, its main export partners were: China (28.3%), the U.S.A. (16.1%) and Canada (6.2%).[19]

25. Peru has signed free trade agreements with the U.S.A., China and the European Free Trade Association among others, opening the way to greater trade and investment with these economies. It is also meant to be a part of the Trans-Pacific Partnership.

26. On April 28, 2011, Peru signed a trade agreement with Chile, Colombia, and Mexico called "La Alianza del Pacífico" ("The Pacific Alliance," in reference to the

15. INEI (2020). *Panorama de la Economía peruana 1950-2019.* INEI. Lima April 2020, https://www.inei.gob.pe/media/MenuRecursivo/publicaciones_digitales/Est/Lib1726/Libro.pdf (accessed Jun. 16, 2021).
16. BCRP. PBI per cápita (S/ 2007), https://bit.ly/3vrYXeR (accessed Jun. 16, 2021).
17. MEF (2021). *Informe anual de deuda pública.* MEF. Lima May 2021, https://bit.ly/3gzIKQP (accessed Jun. 17, 2021).
18. MEF (2021). *Calificaciones de deuda de Largo Plazo Soberana de Países Pares de la región.* MEF. Lima June 2021. https://bit.ly/35tWaHt (accessed Jun. 17, 2021).
19. Trade Map. https://bit.ly/3zKorrs (accessed Jun. 17, 2021).

Pacific Ocean) that rivals Mercosur (formed by Argentina, Brazil, Paraguay, Uruguay, Bolivia and Venezuela) in combined population, GDP, and trade.

27. Its main objective is to become a platform of *political*, economic and commercial integration, with special emphasis on establishing wider bonds with the Asia-Pacific Region.

28. Peru's currency is denominated the "Sol." The exchange rate as of July 16, 2021 is 3.8983 soles to the U.S. dollar.[20]

II. Economy and Competition

29. Before 1990, the Peruvian economy's engine was not a private competition but the Estate's direction, which consisted in high protectionism and direct intervention. In 1963, the government adopted the import-substitution industrialization program, which consisted of developing the local industries by restricting the importation of goods that would compete with local production. Moreover, in 1968 military government, the Estate started to play a central role in production by taking control and by nationalizing natural resources companies, such as oil and mining industries, which are key sectors of the Peruvian economy. Until 1990, the state also owned all the public services companies such as ENTEL and CPT, the telecommunication operators, or the national energy suppliers, such as ELECTROPERU. Furthermore, the State also had a price control policy, mostly used as a populist measure, which exploded during the worst crisis in Peruvian history during the latest 1980s.

30. Indeed, the heterodox economic policy of the government during 1985–1990 and the intern political conflict due to the terrorist movement *SenderoLuminoso* led to the model's debacle. This can be reflected in the worst peak of inflation in Peruvian history (1990, 7649.6%)[21] and the urgent market-oriented reforms applied by the newly elected government of that year.

31. Alberto Fujimori's government followed the World Bank's and the Washington Consensus guidelines and changed the economic model. The market was liberalized in order to attract foreign investors and to impulse the competition of local enterprises; state-owned natural resources and public services industries were reorganized and privatized; and the state's intervention in economy was restricted. These reforms were consolidated in the 1993 new Constitution that followed Fujimori's self-coup d'etat and the closure of the Parliament.

---

20. SBS (2021). *Cotización de oferta y demanda tipo de cambio promedio ponderado*. SBS, https://bit.ly/3vFbkEp (accessed Jun. 17, 2021).
21. *Source*: BCRP, Memoria 1990 (p. 19). https://www.bcrp.gob.pe/docs/Publicaciones/Memoria/1990/Memoria-BCRP-1990-1.pdf .

32. The liberal reforms were included in the economic chapter of the 1993 Constitution. This model is known as "Social Market Economy," although it is different from the original German definition. The economy is now led by the private initiative, by free prices fixed through offer and demand of products and by the competition between private firms. However, the State was relegated to the role of supervising the proper functioning of the market, rather than being an agent with direct intervention.

33. The role of the State in the economy is delimited by the principle of subsidiarity, by which it shall not intervene unless privates cannot and will not be able to satisfy a social demand. When it happens, the State shall apply the less intrusive measure depending on the case.

34. A particular example is the role of the State as a technical regulator of natural monopolies, such as the electrical markets of transmission and distribution, on which a situation of competition must be emulated. However, the State must progressively introduce competition in these markets, for example, as in the telecom market, which has become more competitive during the years due to the introduction of new technologies and the increase in demand.

35. The most representative example of economic supervision is the implementation of a competition policy with the enactment of 1991 Antitrust Act and the creation of National Institute for the Defense of Competition and Protection of Intellectual Property (hereinafter "INDECOPI," for its acronym in Spanish) in 1992, a technical and autonomous institution that supervises free competition and imposes sanctions against the agents who disturb it. Peruvian competition policy prohibits cartels, collusions and abuse of dominant position. However, there is no general restriction or regulations of mergers or concentrations, except for the mergers control in the electrical market.

36. The market-oriented reforms of the 1990s, the promotion of private initiative and free international trade, the impulse on foreign investment in key infrastructure projects and the free competition policy have had a positive impact on constant production growth, more jobs, technology, prices and wealth until now.

37. This can be reflected in the constant economic growth during the past twenty years (excluding the period affected by the COVID-19 pandemic which started in Peru in March 2020) (*see* Figure 1).

Figure 1 GDP: Peru (Annual % Growth)

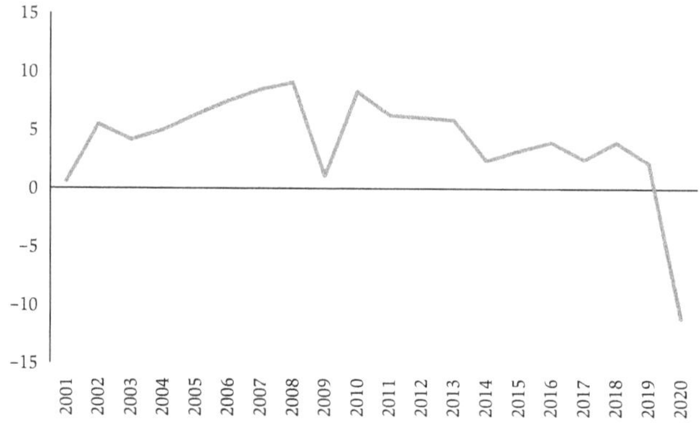

Source: BCRP.

38. The economic system has also worked as a constant impulse for investment, as reflected in Figure 2.

Figure 2 Private Investment: Peru (Constant 2007 Billion S/)

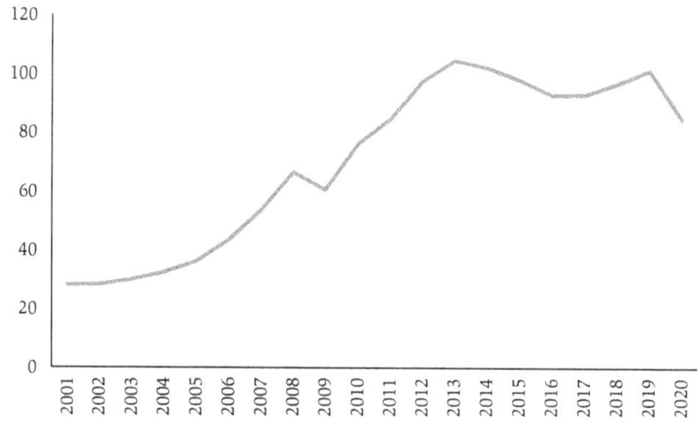

Source: BCRP.

39. These statistics show that the economic reforms, the promotion of competition and the antitrust policy have had a positive effect on the society and the economy since the decade of 1990 up until now. It is worth noting that recently the financial crisis, the political conflicts and the pandemic have significantly affected the growth of private investment in the country.

40. However, the accumulated progress of the reforms might be at stake due to the assumption of the presidency by Pedro Castillo who represents a radical left-wing party. His government program proposes many structural reforms. One of them is changing the economic model to a so-called popular market economy. Although the scope and implications of this model are not clear, a more active intervention of the government in the economy is expected.

41. Mr. Castillo's assumption of the presidency might be explained by the discontent of many people due to the political, economic and health crises. It is important to mention that the political crisis began in 2016 with the presidency of Pedro Pablo Kuczynski due to the constant confrontation with the Congress. Kuczynski resigned in March 2018 and his Prime Minister, Martín Vizcarra assumed the presidency, but the confrontations remained.

42. Due to the conflicts, Vizcarra dissolved the congress in September 2019 and a new congress was installed. In November 2020, Vizcarra was impeached by the new congress due to alleged corruption actions during the time he acted as Regional Governor. Francisco Sagasti, congressman of the center-right political party *Partido Morado* then assumed the presidency for the transitory period, up until July 2021, when Pedro Castillo is to assume the presidency for the next five years.

43. During pandemic, and the effects of a deficient public health system, this political crisis has had a negative impact on the economy and investment levels, as shown in Figures 1 and 2.

§3. Legal System

44. The first Peruvian Constitution was enacted in 1823, two years after the country's independence. Peru has had twelve Constitutions throughout its history, the last one from 1993, which is strongly influenced by libertarian principles that can be explained in the economic and social context of the country in those years (hyperinflation, terrorism, poverty). Peruvian constitution is based on the protection of human rights, with positive impacts on the social and political evolution of the country. From people's side, the full recognition of human and constitutional rights allowed the development of an environment for human relationships, peace and economic growth. On the other hand, on government's side, it establishes limits to the authorities, guaranteeing the protection of private interests over public interventions.

45. Peru has a civil law system, in which the primary legal source is the Civil Code, enacted in 1984. New bills must be approved by the Congress and promulgated by the President. Nevertheless, the Congress can authorize the Executive Power to legislate directly about any matter. Precedents are not common in Peruvian Legal System, although in the past years the courts began to pay attention to the Constitutional Tribunal decisions about the interpretation of the Constitution (only a few of them are considered Precedents).

46. The Constitutional Tribunal is an autonomous and independent entity formed by seven members elected for five years by the Congress. This court has the mission of reviewing the contradictions or oppositions between laws and the Peruvian Constitution. Also, it has to make the final judgments in trials about the affectation of the constitutional rights.

47. The Judicial System, usually known as Judicial Power, is a self-governing organization composed of a hierarchical organization of institutions that exercise the power of administering justice.

48. The Judicial Power is headed by the Supreme Court that has jurisdiction over the whole nation. The second level is composed of the Superior Courts which have jurisdiction over an entire Judicial District. Nowadays, there are thirty-one Judicial Districts in Peru. The third hierarchical level is formed by the Courts of First Instance or, also called, trial courts, which have jurisdiction over each province. Finally, the fourth and lower hierarchical level is made up of the Courts of Peace, which have jurisdiction only over a single district.[22] The Constitution guarantees the right to the double instance.[23]

49. "*ConsejoNacional de la Magistratura*" is in charge of the selection and evaluation of judges.[24] There is also a Public Prosecutor and a Public Defender. The Public Prosecutor has the duty to represent the public interest and defend the rule of law.

50. The predecessor to the Judicial Power in Peru was the "Real Audiencia," which was established during the rule of the Viceroyalty of Peru. At that time, there were many subdivisions which equal to almost to all South American countries with Spanish heritage, with Peru being the center of the legal system.[25] When Peru achieved independence, Jose de San Martin created the "Court of Appeals" with the finality of replacing the "Real Audiencia" and establishing a specific jurisdiction over the northern regions of Peru.

51. Later, Simon Bolivar created the first intent of the legal system as we know it, with the creation of the Superior Court of Justice of Lima, the Superior Court of Justice of Cusco, the Superior Court of Justice of La Libertad and the Superior Court of Justice of Huamanga.[26]

---

22. Judicial Power Official Website, *History and Organisation*, http://historico.pj.gob.pe/conocenos.asp?tema=historia (accessed Jul. 23, 2013).
23. Constitution, Art. 139, 6.
24. Constitution, Art. 154.
25. Recopilación de las Leyes de Indias. *Titulo Quince. De las Audiencias y Cancillerías Reales de las Indias* (1680). View more: http://www.leyes.congreso.gob.pe/Documentos/LeyIndia/0102015.pdf; http://www.congreso.gob.pe/ntley/Imagenes/LeyIndia/0102015.pdf (accessed Sep. 1, 2013).
26. Judicial Power Official Website, *History and Organisation*, http://historico.pj.gob.pe/cortesuprema/cepj/museo_pj/WEB-LA%20JOYA%20DE%20LA%20JUSTICIA/CAPIT%20II.htm (accessed Aug. 27, 2013).

I. Peruvian Courts

A. The Supreme Court

52. The Supreme Court is the highest judicial court in Peru. Its jurisdiction extends over the entire territory of the nation. It is headquartered in the Palace of Justice in Lima. The Supreme Court is composed of three Supreme Sectors:

(1) Civil Sector: Presides over all topics related to civil rights and commercial law.
(2) Criminal Sector: Presides over all topics related to criminal law.
(3) Constitutional and Social Sector: Presides over all topics related to constitutional rights and labor law.

B. The Superior Court

53. The Superior Courts are the second-highest courts of the Judicial System. There is one court for each Judicial District which more or less corresponds with each of the twenty-five regions of Peru. Nowadays, there are thirty-one Judicial Districts that count with a court. A Superior Court is subdivided into smaller courts according to its specialty:

- Civil Courts.
- Criminal Courts.
- Labour Courts.
- Family Courts.
- Commercial Courts.

54. Each court is made up of five justices, one of them being the President of the court. The President of the entire Superior Court is elected between the presidents of each individual court.

§4. Historical Background of Antitrust Law

I. Legislative Decree No. 701

55. Competition law and policy were formally introduced in Peru in 1991 with the enactment of the Legislative Decree No. 701. It was consolidated with the establishment of a duty to protect free competition at constitutional level in the Peruvian Constitution of 1993 and with the opening, in the same year, of a new autonomous governmental agency, the INDECOPI, which is responsible for enforcing antitrust, unfair competition, consumer protection, advertising, bankruptcy and market access laws as well as intellectual property protection. INDECOPI is a governmental agency with technical, administrative, economic and budgetary autonomy. It enforces antitrust laws in all sectors except for telecommunications, where jurisdiction rests on the sector regulator, OSIPTEL (the "*Supervisory Agency of Private Investment in Telecommunications*," OSIPTEL for its acronym in Spanish).

56. Article 3 of Legislative Decree No. 701 prohibited conducts that could be classified as an abuse of dominance or any other that could limit, restrict or distort competition in a way that would affect general economic interest within the territory of Peru. Conducts classified by Article 5 as an "abuse of dominance" were the following: (i) refusal to deal, (ii) price discrimination, (iii) bundling and tying, or (iv) other conducts with an equivalent effect.

57. Legislative Decree No. 701 also prohibited cartels, agreements, decisions, recommendations, parallel conduct or any other concerted practice between undertakings that could limit, restrict or distort competition. Conducts classified by Article 6 as "concerted practices" were the following: (i) price-fixing, (ii) market Allocation, (iii) production allocation, (iv) quality fixing, (v) condition discrimination, (vi) refusal to deal, (vii) bid-rigging cartels, or (viii) other conducts with an equivalent effect.

58. Infringement of Article 3, 5 or 6 was sanctioned through the imposition of fines. For minor and serious infringements, a maximum fine of 1,000 Tax Unit (UIT) (approx. USD 1.07 million) with an upper limit of 10% of the undertaking's brute income from the previous year. For very serious infringements, the upper limit of any fine is established at 10% of the undertaking's brute income from the previous year.

59. It is important to mention that, until the enactment of Legislative Decree No. 788 in 1994, Article 7 allowed concerted practices to exist under the specific approval from the Ministry of Industry's Antitrust Commission,[27] if they were justified as a way to: (i) improve production or commercialization that could not restrict competition, (ii) protect or promote national exporting capacity, (iii) adjust supply to a constant decrease in demand or an excess in production, or (iv) to improve living conditions in depressed economic sectors or geographical areas. The Legislative Decree No. 788 eliminated the power of any authority to give this kind of exception.

60. As the main institution in charge of enforcing antitrust laws, INDECOPI set the trends and main developments in the area in the fifteen years the Legislative Decree No. 701 was in force, creating a system of binding precedents where decisions declared as such were published as de facto rules complementing the very basic statutory definitions. Most of these precedents gave birth to Legislative Decree No. 1034, as explained below.

27. *Comisión Multisectorial de Libre Competencia*, authority in charge of enforcing competition law before INDECOPI was created in 1993.

II. Legislative Decree No. 1034: LRCA

61. Legislative Decree No. 701 was in force for over fifteen years before it was replaced in June 2008 with the Law for the Repression of Anticompetitive Conduct, approved by Legislative Decree No. 1034 (hereinafter "LRCA," for its acronym in Spanish). This new competition law was enacted with the purpose of making the current legislation compatible with the Free Trade Agreement entered into by Peru and the United States of America.

62. Many of the rules developed by INDECOPI through its precedents during the previous years were included as rules in the LRCA. This new law aimed at protecting the antitrust regulations from political interference. Several events warned that the agency had insufficient safeguards of its autonomy and showed that basic statutory definitions allowed for a broad range of discretion for the competition agencies and their officials.

63. The conducts characterized as anticompetitive under the LRCA are consistent with the conducts characterized as anticompetitive in other jurisdictions (abuse of dominant position and vertical and horizontal concerted practices). Recently, a merger control legislation was enacted through Law No. 31112, as explained below.

64. Peruvian competition law follows the European model. Attention is centered on public interest concerns, which are discussed in administrative proceedings. The law focuses on public instruments and agents rather than on private actions or instruments. The enforcement of the law and compliance are basically achieved by the imposition of administrative sanctions. However, in 2020, Law No. 31040 was enacted to reintroduce criminal sanctions for anticompetitive conduct.

65. Even though antitrust damages actions are contemplated in the LRCA, they have not had an important role in this model. While INDECOPI has no authority to award damages directly, in 2018, the LRCA was amended by Legislative Decree No. 1396 to grant the Commission the power to file damages lawsuits of anticompetitive conducts on behalf of the diffuse and collective interests of consumers. In order to do so, a prior report by the Technical Secretariat is issued recommending such action. Even when administrative proceedings brought before INDECOPI may be initiated at a private party's request and that the requesting party may claim and prove antitrust injury, these proceedings are not private antitrust actions. Neither INDECOPI nor OSIPTEL have the authority to award damages.

66. On the other hand, there is no direct private action before courts. Jurisdiction of the competition agency is exclusive, not allowing individuals to resort before or simultaneously to any other administrative authority or court before the exhaustion of such proceedings. In addition, the law does not encourage damages actions with measures such as punitive or treble damages. Private actions are restricted even within proceedings brought before INDECOPI. These proceedings are always initiated ex officio, whether or not a private party has filed a complaint. According to the LRCA, in such cases, the complainant is limited to acting as a "collaborator" of the investigations.

67. One of the most important changes made with the enactment of the LRCA was the clarification as to the objective of Peruvian competition law itself. According to Article 1 of the LRCA, its objective is to "prohibit and sanction anticompetitive behaviour as a means to promote economic efficiency on markets in order to achieve consumer welfare." Even though the LRCA sets its goal as the achievement of "consumer welfare," it clarifies that the means to that goal should follow economic efficiency.

68. As explained below, an improvement included in the LRCA was the imposition of two different standards: "the Per Se Rule" (absolute prohibition) and "the rule of reason" (relative prohibition). Under the absolute prohibition standard, INDECOPI needs to only prove the existence of the conduct, but under the relative prohibition standard, INDECOPI needs to prove that it also restricts competition and has negative effects on consumer welfare. According to the LRCA, all conducts classified as abuse of dominance and some conducts classified as concerted practices fall under the relative prohibition standard. Only those "inter-brand" horizontal agreements which seek to: (i) fix prices or commercial conditions, (ii) restrict or allocate production or sale, or (iii) allocate clients, suppliers or geographic markets; and are not ancillary to other licit agreements, will fall under the absolute prohibition standard.

69. Another important improvement from Legislative Decree No. 701 is the definition set forth in Article 6.2 of the LRCA regarding product market definition. According to this article, product market definition should be assessed taking into consideration possible demand substitution (clients or consumers.

70. Since its enactment, the LRCA has been amended twice, by Legislative Decree No. 1205 and Legislative Decree No. 1396. Given all these amendments, the Unique Consolidated Text of the LRCA was issued by Supreme Decree No. 030-2019-PCM, which will be referred to hereinafter as "LRCA" indistinctly.

71. Legislative Decree No. 1205, published in September 2015 introduced the concept of "facilitator" or "intermediary" as an economic agent subject to the provisions of the LRCA, thus allowing the sanctioning of natural or legal persons serving as facilitators within hub-and-spoke conspiracies. It also clarified the applicable rules for settlement proposals and for the granting of the leniency benefits for cartel participants seeking to collaborate with the authority.

72. Additionally, Legislative Decree No. 1396, published in September 2018 introduced the first whistle-blower program in the Latin American region by establishing monetary rewards for individuals who did not take part in the cartel but can provide information regarding its existence. It also introduced the Commission's power to file damages lawsuits in representation of the diffuse and collective interests of consumers. Prior to the amendment, INDECOPI's Management Board had the power to file such claims.

III. Law No. 26876, Act Against Monopoly and Oligopoly in the Electricity Sector and the New Law No. 31112, Merger Control Act

73. Law No. 26876, Act Against Monopoly and Oligopoly in the Electricity Sector, and the Supreme Decree No. 017-98-ITINCI, was enacted in 1997 and was the prior and sole authorization regime for vertical or horizontal mergers, acquisitions, or any kind of economic concentration. As its title entails, it was only applicable to operations in the electricity market. Any horizontal concentration that may accumulate 15% or more of the market's share or any vertical concentration that may accumulate 5% or more of the share shall be subject to the Commission of Free Competition's prior authorization, even if it originated or took place in foreign territory.

74. In the span of more than twenty years after it came into effect, twenty cases were notified, and only three of them were subject to conditions for approval.

75. A new merger control law of general scope was approved in January 2021 through Law No. 31112. Law No. 31112 entered into force on June 14, 2021, thus repelling the special provisions applicable to the electricity sector.

Part I. The Structure of Antitrust Law and Its Enforcement

Chapter 1. Sources of Antitrust Law in Peru

§1. INTRODUCTION

76. The main set of norms that govern the general antitrust policy in Peru is contained in the LRCA and most recently in Law No. 31112. It is important to mention that the decisions of INDECOPI's instances also play an important role in the interpretation and application of such act, giving it content and a regular methodology of the conduct's analysis.

77. INDECOPI's organization, functions and faculties are regulated by Legislative Decree No. 807, Legislative Decree No. 1033 and its Regulations, Supreme Decree No. 009-2009-PCM, which readjusted the competition agency's structure to achieve more guarantees for the citizens. The Regulations have been partly replaced by INDECOPI's new Organization and Functions Regulations enacted by Supreme Decree No. 104-2021-PCM, which among others, includes additional functions for the Commission and the National Directorate for the Surveillance and Promotion of Competition (NDC).

78. There is also a specific antitrust regulation for the telecom market. Competition law in the telecom market is supervised by a specific bureau of the telecom regulator, OSIPTEL, which oversees applying the LRCA to the telecom operators and imposing sanctions.

79. Last, we must mention that Peru is a member of the Andean Community of Nations (CAN), which is a supranational organization incorporated by Latin-American countries, whose decisions have direct effects on its members' territories. The CAN's competition policy is regulated by the 2005 Decision No. 608 and sanctions agreements and abuse of dominant position that occur or may have effects on more than one country member. To date, there has not been an antitrust case led by the CAN that involved the Peruvian market.

§2. National Sources

I. The Constitution

80. The 1993 Constitution is the country's fundamental norm, which establishes, in its economic chapter, the general principles of the Peruvian free-competition policy, specifically in Article 61:

> The State facilitates and oversees for the free competition. It fights any practice that would limit it, as well as the abuse of dominant or monopolistic positions. No law or agreement shall authorize or establish monopolies. (...).[28]

81. This policy accompanies the new economic model introduced by the market-oriented reforms in Peru during the 1990s. The State is no longer a direct agent or a director of the economy; it just supervises that the market follows the free concurrence of the offer and the demand. Hence, it watches for the consumer surplus not being diminished by a market distortion due to the abuse of an agent with a dominant position. It is not forbidden to achieve a dominant position, but to abuse it.

82. Monopolies are not forbidden when they are achieved through the agent's efficiency and competition. On the contrary, it is forbidden to artificially create a monopoly that distorts a market that functions in a free competitive situation. However, there are obvious exceptions like natural monopolies or patents, which are market structures that work more efficiently as legal and regulated monopolies. Still the State must promote competition in them.

II. Legislative Decree No. 1033: INDECOPI's Organization and Functions

83. Peruvian's INDECOPI is the national competition authority that, among other functions, supervises competition in the market. Its structure, duties and faculties are ruled by the INDECOPI's Organization and Functions Act, Legislative

28. Article 61.—The State facilitates and oversees free competition. It fights any practice that would limit it and the abuse of dominant or monopolistic positions. No law or concealment may authorize or provide monopolies.

Press, radio, television and any other means of social communication, and in general, enterprises, goods and services related to the freedom of expression and communication cannot be the object of exclusivity, monopoly or seizure of goods, direct or indirectly, by the State or private sector.

[Artículo 61.—El Estado facilita y vigila la libre competencia. Combate toda práctica que la limite y el abuso de posiciones dominantes o monopólicas. Ninguna ley ni concertación puede autorizar ni establecer monopolios.

La prensa, la radio, la televisión y los demás medios de expresión y comunicación social; y, en general, las empresas, los bienes y servicios relacionados con la libertad de expresión y de comunicación, no pueden ser objeto de exclusividad, monopolio ni acaparamiento, directa ni indirectamente, por parte del Estado ni de particulares.]

Decree No. 1033, and their Regulations, Supreme Decree No. 009-2009-PCM, introduced as an institutional reform for the implementation of the Free Trade Agreement between Peru and the U.S.A.

84. These norms provide the functions of the offices involved in the investigation and decision-making about antitrust practices: the Technical Secretary, which is the investigating and instructor entity of the procedure; the Antitrust Commission, the first instance, and the Tribunal for the Defense of Competition and Intellectual Property, which is the last administrative instance in charge of unifying the decision criteria.

85. Along with the recent entry into force of Law No. 31112, Merger Control Act, in 2021 INDECOPI's Organization and Functions Regulation was modified to include INDECOPI's new power to carry out the merger control procedure. The new Regulation also introduced a relevant change in INDECOPI's internal organization by assigning all the functions of the Technical Secretary to the newly renamed NDC (formerly, the Commission's Technical Secretariat), dependent on the General Management Office.

86. INDECOPI's Organization and Functions Act and Regulation also establish the election procedures of the bureau's members. In this respect, there are critics about the institutional independence and autonomy, because the president of the board of directors is elected by the President of Peru and the directors are elected by the Ministers. For their part, they elect the members of the decision instances. Therefore, the autonomy guaranties are still weak, and the institution may be prone to political capture.

III. Legislative Decree No. 1034 (LRCA)

87. The core of the antitrust policy in Peru is regulated in the LRCA. This act amended the previous Legislative Decree No. 701, filling some gaps and putting an end to discussions generated by contradictory decisions of INDECOPI's Tribunal in the past.

88. The scope of application includes all the conducts performed in Peru by economic agents: natural persons, private and state-owned companies, associations, trust funds, or any subject that participates in the market by offering or demanding goods and services. The actions taken following, or in compliance with, a legal provision are exceptions to these provisions.

89. Although still ruled by the provisions of the LRCA, the proceedings initiated against companies of the telecom market are followed before their regulation authority, OSIPTEL, which has autonomy and independence in deciding the cases. This power is conferred by the LRCA. Merger control in the telecommunications sector is the only competition-related power that OSIPTEL does not have, as this falls within the exclusive authority of INDECOPI.

90. Competition policy in the LRCA is based on two general prohibitions: (i) the per se prohibition of horizontal agreements and (ii) the rule of reason prohibition of dominant position abuse.

91. This decree also rules the investigation, the compilation of proofs, the administrative sanctioning procedure, interim measures, the sanctions, etc. The LRCA also focuses on the powers of the bodies in charge during the procedure.

IV. Law No. 31112 and Its Regulations

92. In June 2021, Law No. 31112, the Merger Control Act entered into force and repealed the previous merger control established in 1997 by Law No. 26876, which was applicable only to the electricity sector.

93. Under the new act, any transaction that involves transfer or change in the control of an economic agent or part of it, with effects in Peru, is subject to mandatory notification when it surpasses the following thresholds:

(1) the total annual gross sale or income or asset book value in the country of all companies involved during the year prior to filing should be equal or greater than 118,000 Tax Reference Units (UITs, for their acronym in Spanish) (approx. USD 141 million for 2021); and,
(2) the total annual gross sale or income or asset book value in the country of at least two of the companies involved shall be equal or greater than 18,000 UITs (approx. USD 21.5 million for 2021).

94. The new act also confers INDECOPI the power to initiate ex officio investigations for up to one year after the closing of concentrations falling below the thresholds, provided they might potentially restrict competition.

95. INDECOPI's Antitrust Commission is the first instance body in charge of conducting the merger control procedure and the substantive analysis of the concentration, which is aimed at determining whether the transaction might potentially restrict competition in the involved markets. The act expressly prohibits INDECOPI from considering factors not established in the act for the assessment of concentrations (e.g., the impact on the labor market or control of foreign investments).

§3. International Sources

I. CAN Decision No. 608

96. The only international source of antitrust regulation with direct effects in Peru is the 2005 CAN Decision No. 608. It is bidding to all the economic agents (private and state-owned companies, individuals, or non-lucrative associations that offer or demand goods and services) that perform actions against free competition in two or more country members or whose effects may affect the economy in two or more country members. However, the countries may ask the Commission in charge for an exclusion or exception to the application of the Antitrust Decision on sensitive national markets that comply with specific listed requirements.

97. The decision rules the proceeding followed through the CAN instance. The investigation is led by the Technical Secretariat and the decision is taken by the Andean Committee for the Defense of Free Competition, which may impose corrective measures or sanction fees.

98. This provision also establishes the election mechanism for the authorities in charge of the proceeding. The Technical Secretariat, which is the investigating and instructor office, is elected by the General Secretariat of the CAN. On the other hand, the Committee's members are assigned by the antitrust authority of each country member. The Chairman of the Committee is the representative of the same country member of the Andean Presidential Counsel's Chairman.

§4. Secondary Sources

I. Regulations

99. The LRCA compiles the substantive rules for the defense of competition. Thus, there is no regulation that complements those provisions. However, there are still some relevant provisions that have already been mentioned.

100. The main one is INDECOPI's Organization and Functions Regulation, which was recently updated by Supreme Decree No. 104-2021-PCM. It complements the provisions included in the act and provides further detail into the structure of INDECOPI as the competition agency.

101. Given the recent enactment and application of the new Merger Control Act approved in Law No. 31112, the Regulations of said the act also came into force by Supreme Decree No. 039-2021-PCM, which complement and specify the rules and procedures applicable to the new merger control regime.

II. Guidelines

102. In recent years, the Competition Agencies have published several guidelines aimed at providing legal certainty to economic agents regarding the application of certain figures established both in the LRCA and in the Merger Control Act.

103. For instance, in August 2017, INDECOPI's Antitrust Commission published the Leniency Program Guidelines,[29] which develops the requirements established in the LRCA for the application and granting of benefits to cartel participants that denounce their infringement and collaborates with the authority. OSIPTEL followed along with the publication of the Leniency Program Guidelines applicable to the Telecommunications Sector in October 2020.[30]

104. These Guidelines state that the program is aimed at offenders, individuals, or undertakings who provide evidence that helps prove the existence of a cartel and sanction it; and that it does not apply to those who have coerced other agents to comply with the cartel. The Guidelines include three levels of benefits: (i) Type A Leniency (100% exemption of the fine), before the cartel is detected by INDECOPI; (ii) Type B Leniency (reducing the amount of the fine in a range that goes from 50% to a complete exoneration), once the cartel has been detected by INDECOPI; and (iii) Type C Leniency (reduction of up to 50% of the fine), once the administrative sanctioning procedure has been initiated.

105. In December 2019, the Antitrust Commission published the Antitrust Rewards Program Guidelines.[31] This program complements the Leniency Program described above but applies only to individuals who have not participated in the cartel or those who did not have a central role in the cartel and can provide relevant information of its existence (e.g., family members and former employees of the companies under investigation). In that sense, it does not apply to undertakings. In this case, it seeks to facilitate the timely detection, accreditation, and sanction of cartels through payments (i.e., rewards). The Guidelines develop two types of reward amounts: (i) a base amount (of USD 51,000 for 2021, approximately) and a variable amount (determined according to the success of the procedure and the fine imposed on the offender of up to USD 102,000 for 2021, approximately).

106. In April 2021, INDECOPI's Antitrust Commission published the Guidelines on Compensation for Damages Caused to Consumers as a Result of Anti-Competitive Conducts.[32] These establish the criteria that the Antitrust Commission must follow to file a damage claim as a result of anticompetitive conducts in defense of the diffuse or collective interests of consumers affected by the anticompetitive conduct, as well as the corresponding procedural aspects for said purpose.

107. Finally, in May 2021, INDECOPI presented the Threshold Calculation Guidelines,[33] applicable to the threshold calculation for the application of the Merger Control Act. In this sense, it develops the calculation method based on: (i)

29. Available in Spanish at: https://bit.ly/35P8cvz.
30. Available in Spanish at: https://bit.ly/3qyrY7U.
31. Available in English at: https://bit.ly/3dsup6u.
32. Available in Spanish at: https://bit.ly/3wFj3DL.
33. Available in Spanish at: https://bit.ly/3gHvKYd.

the sales or gross income generated by the companies involved in the business concentration operation; or (ii) the value of the assets of the companies involved in the business concentration operation.

108. Among other rules, the Guidelines determine that in the case of income, only the revenue from the ordinary course of business shall be considered; and in the case of assets, all assets located in Peru shall be incorporated in the calculation, except for those that were not located in the country during the year prior to notification and those for which more than 50% of their income come from foreign sales. The document also explains the special provisions for the calculation of notification thresholds in relation to concentrations of financial entities, investment funds, insurance companies and pension funds.

§5. Sources Relation and Hierarchy

109. Legal hierarchy in Peru is very simple. The Constitution is the fundamental law and occupies the top of the pyramid. All other laws and regulations must suit its provisions. However, the Constitution has very general principles and, in the matter of antitrust policy, it is more a command on the State to defend the free competition and to not create artificial monopolies.

110. Although there are discussions about the status of international sources, the Constitution's Articles 55–57 and 200 can be read as giving international antitrust sources a lower status than the Constitution. Also, if an international antitrust source were to modify or eliminate a national law, it would be necessary for a prior Parliament's approval. Hence, the provisions of CAN Decision No. 608 must suit Peru's Constitution and should not directly modify or eliminate any national law.

111. The next position in the hierarchy is occupied by the Congress' Acts, Law Decrees and Legislative Decrees, all of which have the same status. Law Decrees are the government's laws enacted during a coup d'etat and the Legislative Decrees are the laws enacted by the government with a prior authorization of the Parliament. The Antitrust Act in Peru is a Legislative Decree, and it has a lower status than the Constitution.

112. The Regulations enacted by the government complement and give more content to the Parliament's Acts or the Legislative Decrees, without breaching the scope of the latter. They have the lowest hierarchy and must suit all the abovementioned sources' provisions.

§6. Role and Authority of Precedents

113. Peru has a civil law system; thus, its main rules are included in the Parliament or Government's Acts. The administration's agencies, such as INDECOPI or OSIPTEL, can set precedents, but they would only be binding to the same agency.

The Judiciary Supreme Court can set precedents as well, though any court may render a different decision with the only requirement of explaining the reasons.

114. INDECOPI's Organization and Functions Act confers faculties to its Tribunal, which is the higher antitrust authority within the competition agency, to expressly set binding precedents to its lower status commissions. However, they are not binding for OSIPTEL or the judiciary. It is important to consider that even without an express precedent, the Antitrust Commission tends to suit its decision to INDECOPI Tribunal's criteria.

115. The Tribunal has set some important (and some controversial) precedents during the ruling of prior Antitrust Act, Legislative Decree No. 701, related, for example, to the application of the per se and the reason rule prohibition, to the scope of application of the antitrust law or to the Technical Secretary's powers. Since the enactment of the LRCA, there has been only one precedent, about vertical restraints. This decision has been challenged against the judiciary.

Chapter 2. Scope of Application

§1. Territorial Reach

116. According to Article 4 of the LRCA, its rules only apply to restrictions that affect Peruvian territory. It also states that all restrictive actions that have an effect over all or part of Peruvian territory can be targeted by the competition law, even if those conducts originated abroad.[34]

§2. Special Sectors

I. Telecommunications

117. Article 13 of the LRCA establishes that the Peruvian Competition Government Authority is, in the first instance, INDECOPI's Antitrust Commission and, in the second instance, INDECOPI's Tribunal for the Competition Defense and for the Intellectual Property Protection.[35]

118. However, Article 17 establishes that OSIPTEL (Peru's Agency for the Supervision of Private Investment in Telecommunications) will oversee the enforcement of the LRCA in the telecommunications sector.[36]

---

34. Article 4.—Territorial Scope of Application.—

This law applies to conducts that generate or that can generate anticompetitive effects over all or over part of the national territory, even if those conducts are originated abroad.

[Artículo 4.—Ámbito de aplicación territorial.—

La presente Ley es de aplicación a las conductas que produzcan o puedan producir efectos anticompetitivos en todo o en parte del territorio nacional, aun cuando dicho acto se haya originado en el extranjero].

35. Article 13.—The government competition authorities.—

13.1. In first instance, the competition authority is INDECOPI's Commission for the Free Competition Defence.

13.2. In second instance, the competition authority is INDECOPI's Tribunal for the Competition Defence and for the Intellectual Property Protection.

[Artículo 13.—Las autoridades de competencia.—

13.1. En primera instancia administrativa la autoridad de competencia es la Comisión, entendiendo por ésta a la Comisión de Defensa de la Libre Competencia del INDECOPI.

13.2. En segunda instancia administrativa la autoridad de competencia es el Tribunal, entendiendo por éste al Tribunal de Defensa de la Competencia y de la Protección de la Propiedad Intelectual del INDECOPI.]

36. Article 17.—About OSIPTEL.—

The appliance of this Law in the telecommunication public services market will be in charge of the Agency for the Supervision of Private Investment in Telecommunications – OSIPTEL –, according to what has been established by Law No. 27336 that develops OSIPTEL's functions and competences. In that sense, its different instances, their competences and the procedures which guide their actions will be defined in its own legal framework.

[Artículo 17.—Del OSIPTEL.—

La aplicación de la presente Ley al mercado de los servicios públicos de telecomunicaciones estará a cargo del Organismo Supervisor de la Inversión Privada en Telecomunicaciones—OSIPTEL

119. In addition, according to Law No. 27336, that develops OSIPTEL's functions and competences, this agency can enforce the LRCA to sanction companies which are not in the telecommunications sector, but whose actions can affect the telecommunication public services market.[37]

120. Accordingly, even though OSIPTEL remains the authority with powers to enforce the application of the LRCA in the telecommunications sector, it has no power to conduct merger control procedures, given that this is an exclusive power of INDECOPI for all economic sectors.

§3. State-Owned Enterprises and Public Utilities

I. The State's Subsidiary Role

121. According to the Peruvian Constitution, the Peruvian State has a subsidiary role in the country's economy, meaning that it can only become engaged in business activities in case there are no private companies providing goods and services in each market and after it has been authorized by express law, for reasons of high public interest or of manifest national convenience.[38]

---

de conformidad con lo dispuesto en la Ley No. 27336, Ley de Desarrollo de las Funciones y Facultades del OSIPTEL. En tal sentido, las instancias competentes, las facultades de éstas y los procedimientos que rigen su actuación serán los establecidos en su marco normativo].

37. Article 36.—Dispute Resolution Procedure

OSIPTEL has competence to solve any dispute which may arise as a consequence of actions or omissions that affect or might affect the telecommunication public services market, even if only one of the parties has the condition of a telecommunication public services operating company.

[Artículo 36.—Procedimiento de solución de controversias en la vía administrativa

(…) OSIPTEL es competente para conocer de toda controversia que se plantee como consecuencia de acciones u omisiones que afecten o puedan afectar el mercado de los servicios públicos de telecomunicaciones, aunque sólo una de las partes tenga la condición de empresa operadora de tales servicios].

Article 26.—Competition related violations regime and personal sanctions

(…)

26.2 OSIPTEL can sanction any person or legal entity which does not have the condition of a telecommunication public services operating company, for infringing free or fair competition rules in the cases referred to by Art. 36 (…).

[Artículo 26.—Régimen de infracciones relacionadas con competencia y sanciones personales

(…)

26.2 OSIPTEL podrá sancionar a las personas naturales o jurídicas que no tengan la condición de operadoras de servicios públicos de telecomunicaciones, por incumplimiento de las normas de libre y leal competencia, en los casos a que se refiere, el último párrafo del Artículo 36 de la presente Ley (… .).]

38. Article 60.—The State recognizes economic pluralism. The national economy is sustained in the coexistence of diverse forms of ownership and enterprise.

Authorized solely by express law, the State may subsidiarily engage in business activities, directly or indirectly, for reasons of high public interest or manifest national convenience.

Business activity receives the same legal treatment, whether public or private.

[Artículo 60.—El Estado reconoce el pluralismo económico. La economía nacional se sustenta en la coexistencia de diversas formas de propiedad y de empresa.

122. Peruvian state-owned companies went through an intense privatization process in the last decade of the past century. Despite this process, several state-owned companies remain in different economic sectors.

123. State-owned enterprises are governed by the same rules as other private agents.

II. Energy Sector

124. Petróleos del Perú (Petroperú) is a state-owned Peruvian petroleum company dedicated to the transportation, refinance, distribution and commercialization of fuels and other petroleum-derived products. It was created on June 24, 1969, after former Peruvian president, Juan Velasco Alvarado, nationalized the Standard Oil Petroleum Company.

125. Electroperú is also a state-owned company that was created on September 5, 1972, and that participates in the generation of electric energy. It owns two hydroelectric stations which are part of the Mantaro Hydroelectric complex, the country's most important electric generation center.

126. It is important to point out that several power generators are owned by private companies and that, in recent years, the construction and administration of numerous electric transmission lines have been granted to private companies.

127. While two privately owned companies provide and distribute power to the capital city of Lima, most household power distribution in the country remains mostly state-owned through a series of regional companies.

III. Water

128. SEDAPAL is a state-owned company that was created by Congress Law on June 12, 1981. It provides sanitation services such as drinkable water and the sewage system and is in charge of the operation, maintenance, control and development of those basic services in the Provinces of Lima and Callao.

IV. Banking and Finance

129. *Banco de la Nación* is a state-owned bank that was created by Congress Law on January 27, 1966. It is part of the Peruvian State's economy and finance

---

Sólo autorizado por ley expresa, el Estado puede realizar subsidiariamente actividad empresarial, directa o indirecta, por razón de alto interés público o de manifiesta conveniencia nacional.

La actividad empresarial, pública o no pública, recibe el mismo tratamiento legal].

sector. It oversees the administration of the Public Treasury's subaccounts, and it provides the Central Government with basic services for the administration of public funds such as tax collection.

130. However, it is important to notice that most of these basic services can also be provided by private-owned financial institutions, which means that the State is breaching its constitutional subsidiary role. As of 2021, there have been several legislative initiatives to further the activities of this financial entity.

§4. Sensible Effect and *De Minimis*

131. The LRCA does not establish a *de minimis* or a substantial trade restriction rule, meaning that violations of this law must be analyzed case by case, evaluating the affected market's special characteristics (e.g., its high concentration or vertical integration level) and taking into account structural and dynamic factors.

132. However, the Peruvian Competition Authority (INDECOPI) has aimed to include a *de minimis* or a substantial trade restriction rule in some of its decisions. For example, in *Depósito Santa Beatriz v. Distribuidora Norte Pacasmayo*, dated 2003, the Antitrust Commission resolved that one of the requirements to verify an anticompetitive practice was to have evidence of the affection of a "non-insubstantial" portion of the market, formal requirement that intends to quantify the extent to which the market has been affected by the investigated practice.[39]

133. Some years later, in *Aero Servicios* (an airplane fuel retail seller) *v. Petróleos del Perú* (a State company dedicated to the production and distribution of fuels), dated 2010, the Commission considered that even if Petróleos del Perú's refusal to sell Turbo Jet A1 fuel to Aero Servicios could affect this company, the compromised Turbo Jet A1 Jet fuel retail sales only represented 0.2% of the supposedly affected market and this percentage was not enough in order to consider that competition could be distorted in this market.[40]

134. Recently, in 2013, in *OSIPTEL v. Telefónica del Perú*, OSIPTEL pointed out that the LRCA does not establish a *de minimis* rule. According to this governmental entity, adopting a *de minimis* rule in highly concentrated markets, in which very few agents participate, could imply discarding the enforcement of the competition law in those markets.[41]

39. Resolution No. 006-2003-INDECOPI/CLC.
40. Resolution No. 009-2010/CLC-INDECOPI.
41. Resolution No. 004-2013-TSC/OSIPTEL.

Chapter 3. Overview of Substantive Provisions

§1. Restrictive Agreements

135. Articles 8 and 9 of the LRCA have determined that the prohibition of certain behaviors can be absolute or relative. In cases of absolute prohibitions, to verify the existence of the breach, it is sufficient that the competition authority proves the existence of an illegal behavior. On the contrary, in cases of relative prohibitions, to verify the existence of breach, INDECOPI should prove that the existence of the conduct has or may have a negative effect on competition.

I. Article 11 of the LRCA

136. According to Article 11.2, only naked-horizontal cartels have absolute prohibition. They are punishable per se if the agreement is to:

(1) establish prices or other trade or service conditions;
(2) limiting production or sales, especially by shares;
(3) allocate customers, suppliers or geographical areas;
(4) establish positions or abstentions in bids, tenders or other contractual forms or public acquisition under the current legislation.

137. Other forms of horizontal agreements have relative prohibition, and they are analyzed by the "Rule of Reason." This happens, for example, with the collaboration agreements. The INDECOPI and the Peruvian doctrine have interpreted those cases in the light of the ancillary doctrine. In the binding precedent "*Miguel Ciccia Vásquez E.I.R.L. (Civa) v. Empresa de Turismo Mariscal Cáceres S.A.*," the Tribunal provided that the agreements to establish prices and allocate the market will be illegal per se only if their object is to restrict competition, but if the agreement complements an association with the object to generate efficiency in the market, they should be analyzed by the "Rule of Reason" in order to determine their rationality.

138. The rest of the illegal behaviors identified by the LRCA, like vertical agreements or abuse of dominance, are considered relative prohibitions as well.

§2. Dominant Undertakings

139. According to Article 1, the object of the LRCA is to forbid and punish anticompetitive behavior to promote economic efficiency in all markets to guarantee the consumer's well-being.

I. Article 7 of the LRCA

140. Article 7 of the LRCA establishes the criteria that must be used by the authority in order to determine if an agent has a dominant position (market power), which is defined as the possibility of distorting, restricting or affecting the supply or demand conditions in a specific relevant market, without the possibility for its competitors, suppliers or clients to limit this situation in this moment or in a short term.

141. Article 7.1 states that when analyzing the existence of dominant position, the authority will take into consideration not only the agent's market share but also the characteristics of the supply and the demand of the goods or services, the technological development or services involved, the possibility for competitors to access to financing and supply sources and distribution logistics, the existence of entry barriers and the existence of suppliers, clients, competitors with enough negotiation power.

142. Having a dominant position is not considered illegal. According to Article 7.1 of the LRCA, a conduct will only be sanctioned as an abuse of dominant position when a firm uses its power to restrict competition, obtain benefits and harm actual or potential, direct or indirect competitors. The LRCA requires that abuses of dominant position have an exclusionary effect (there are no sections for the so-called exploitative practices) and can consist of conducts such as refusals to deal, discrimination practices, tying, limiting market access or membership to organizations and associations, exclusive distribution or exclusive dealing, non-competition agreements, abuse of judicial and other governmental proceedings (sham litigation) and, in general, of any conduct that may harm or limit competition for reasons other than efficiency.

§3. Concentrations

I. The Current Status Quo: New Merger Control Act

143. Law No. 31112, a new "Merger Control Act," is applicable to all sectors of the economy. Its Regulations were approved by Supreme Decree No. 039-2021-PCM. Both came into force as of June 14, 2021.

144. The new framework replaces the previous merger control regime, established by Law No. 26876, "Act Against Monopoly and Oligopoly in the Electricity Sector," which provided for a premerger authorization requirement applicable only to the electricity sector.

145. The Merger Control Act establishes that operations involving a transfer or change in the control of an undertaking or part of it, resulting from any of the following transactions, shall be notified before their closing takes place, provided they meet the following thresholds:

(a) The total sum of the value of annual sales or gross income or the value of the assets in the country of the companies involved in the concentration during the fiscal year prior to notification should be equal to or greater than 118,000 Tax Reference Units, approximately USD 141 million in 2021.
(b) The value of the annual sales or gross income or the value of the assets in the country of at least two of the companies involved in the concentration during the fiscal year prior to notification should be each equal to or greater than 18,000 Tax Reference Units, approximately USD 21.5 million in 2021.

146. INDECOPI's Antitrust Commission is the first instance body responsible for conducting the merger control procedure and the substantive analysis of the concentration, which is aimed at determining whether the transaction might potentially restrict competition in the involved markets. The act expressly prohibits INDECOPI from considering factors not established in it for the assessment of concentrations (e.g., the impact on the labor market or control of foreign investments).

§4. Other Prohibitions

147. Other than those stated above, there are no other prohibitions in the LRCA.

§5. Tests of Illegality

148. There are two kinds of illegality tests in the LRCA, depending on the nature of the conduct analyzed: the absolute prohibitions and the relative prohibitions.

I. Per Se Prohibitions and Naked Restraints (Absolute Prohibitions under LRCA)

149. The concept of the absolute prohibition (also known as naked agreements) is regulated in Article 8 of the LRCA: "In cases of absolute prohibition, to verify the existence of the administrative infringement, it is sufficient that the competition authority proves the existence of the behaviour." In this type of prohibition, the infringing party is punished without analyzing the benefits and harms that are generated in the market. Absolute prohibitions objectively restrict development of certain behaviors which generate anticompetitive effects. This is known as the Per Se Rule. Confirming the existence of the behavior is enough for the authority to punish the offender.

150. With respect to the Per Se Rule, it should be analyzed that its application as an evaluation criterion was established in Peru for the first time as a ruling of mandatory compliance by the INDECOPI's Tribunal in *Civa v. EmpresaTurística-MariscalCáceres S.A.* (hereinafter *CasoCiva*), resolved by means of Resolution No.

206-97-TDC/INDECOPI dated October 28, 1997.[42] This was confirmed later by the INDECOPI's Tribunal Resolution No. 276-97-TDC/INDECOPI dated November 27, 1997. This last resolution was issued within the framework of the ex officio procedure initiated by the Antitrust Commission of INDECOPI against the Asociación Peruana de Avicultura and others for the alleged arrangement of prices, commercialization conditions and chicken volume of production.[43]

151. Currently, the Peruvian legislation on competition unequivocally establishes the cases in which a conduct is deemed as per se illegal:

> Article 11 of Legislative Decree 1034:
> (...)
>
> 11.2. Horizontal Collusive practices are those practices, decisions, recommendations or concerted practices used by economic agents competing among them that have the purpose or effect of restricting, preventing or distorting free competition ...

---

42. The case involved a Transport Agency Services Agreement whereby Mariscal Cáceres Company agreed to lease part of its facilities at a bus terminal to CIVA and other companies to provide cargo and passengers transportation services. The lease agreement contained a submission to the Terminal Internal Regulations which included the division of routes and price fixing by the terminal Administration. CIVA filed a complaint against "its partners" at the terminal alleging that the agreement in essence was a price cartel and market division.

In analyzing the case, INDECOPI's Tribunal in its Resolution No. 206-97-TDC/INDECOPI stated:

> (...) naked agreements are deemed illegal per se since their purpose and effect is to restrict the production and consequently restrict competition. These agreements are referred to in Article 6, a) and b) of Legislative Decree No. 701.
>
> On the other hand, those accessory or complementary agreements that somehow reduce competition between companies are not deemed per se illegal since they may involve integration in a particular productive activity and as such have the ability to create efficiency and reduce costs in favor of the consumer. In that case you cannot really speak of an agreement to fix prices or market allocation but of an association agreement, "joint venture" or other form of productive integration.
>
> (...)
>
> In this regard, price fixing and market allocation agreements will be deemed per se illegal when they are not a consequence of nor form part of an integration contract or are not effective to achieve efficiency from such integration. What is intended to explain here is that such agreements jump the per se illegal barrier so their legality must be analysed from the perspective of the "rule of reason."

43. In the referred Resolution INDECOPI's Tribunal established as a previous ruling of mandatory compliance the following:

> Pursuant to the rules contained in Legislative Decree 701, prices fixing, market share distribution, production quota distribution and restriction or control of production must be punished according to the "per se" rule. This implies that the mere use of the forbidden practice constitutes an administrative offense that must be punished as provided by law. In that line, to configure the violation, it is not necessary to consider the damage that the practice may cause to the market or its reasonability, that is, whether it may produce or not the mentioned negative effects.

a) To fix prices or other commercial or service conditions;
b) To limit production or sales particularly through market shares;
c) To distribute customers, suppliers or geographic areas; or,
d) To establish positions or abstentions in bids, tenders or other form of public contracting or acquisition, as well as in public auctions, provided by the applicable law.

152. As noted, under the current logic of the Antitrust Legislation, "naked" agreements among competitors, that is, those who have direct and exclusive purpose of restricting competition (price agreements, market sharing, establishment of commercial conditions, etc.), are per se illegal. In all other cases the rule of reason is applied, so that an agreement between competitors would be illegal only to the extent it affects competition unreasonably.

Article 11 of Legislative Decree No. 1034:
(…)

11.3. Horizontal collusive practices other than those described in paragraph 11.2 above are relative prohibitions.

II. Balancing Tests (Relative Prohibitions)

153. The concept of relative prohibition is regulated in Article 9 of the LRCA: "In the relative prohibitions to verify the existence of the administrative infringement, the competition authority must prove the existence of the conduct and that it has, or it could have, negative effects on competition and consumer welfare." In the cases analyzed under this scheme it is necessary to prove not only the existence of behavior but also the existence of an exclusionary effect.

154. The relative prohibitions follow the "Rule of Reason," restricting certain conducts only if they generate or may generate anticompetitive effects on the market in the case. Anticompetitive effects suffered by a competitor derived from the practice do not constitute an infringement, requiring that market effects on consumer welfare and general competition also be pondered in each case.

155. All practices typified in the LRCA which have not been explicitly considered as absolute prohibitions are governed by the rule of reason. These are:

(a) The practices of abuse of dominant position.
(b) The horizontal agreements other than those mentioned in the absolute prohibitions, or the agreements, decisions or concerted practices recommendations made by competitors that have the object or effect of restricting or distorting competition.
(c) The vertical collusive practices.

156. The rule of reason is applied, among other cases, when agreements that restrict competition are ancillary to larger lawful agreements whose purpose is not to restrict competition (e.g., business collaboration agreements). This exemption is known as the "*ancillary doctrine*" or complementary doctrine, according to which the only agreements that will be subject to the application of the Per Se Rule will be those whose sole purpose is to restrict competition—the so-called naked agreements.

157. In Peru, ancillary doctrine was included for the first time by INDECOPI's Tribunal in the already mentioned CIVA case.[44] For the application of the ancillary doctrine, the authority usually adopts a scheme of analysis coincident with the American criteria which are reflected in the doctrine applicable to the rules for the promotion of free competition:

- It must be determined that the agreement is essential for the integration activity. If so, the agreement shall be deemed valid and lawful. Otherwise, the agreement must be subject to the analysis described in the next points.
- Price-fixing or market allocation agreements must be referred to an economic activity jointly developed, for example, joint provision of a specific service or joint production or commercialization of a good by two agents.
- The market share for each member participating in the agreement must not pose risks to competition.
- The parties to the agreement shall not have as main purpose or intention the restriction of competition.

158. Within this scheme, the ancillary doctrine serves as an element to counteract the presumption of illegality that weighs against this type of practice. If they have been used within the framework of a larger integration agreement, the evaluation by the competent authority shall be less strict because in such cases there is the possibility that these practices may generate efficiency.

---

44. Resolution No. 206-97-TDC/INDECOPI dated Aug. 13, 1997, published at the official gazette *El Peruano* on Oct. 28, 1997. In this regard, INDECOPI's Tribunal stated:

> (...) naked agreements are deemed illegal per se since their purpose and effect is to restrict the production and consequently restrict competition. These agreements are referred to in Article 6, a) and b) of Legislative Decree No. 701.
>
> On the other hand, those accessory or complementary agreements that somehow reduce competition between companies are not deemed per se illegal since they may involve integration in a particular productive activity and as such have the ability to create efficiency and reduce costs in favor of the consumer. In that case you cannot really speak of an agreement to fix prices or market allocation but of an association agreement, "joint venture" or other form of productive integration.
>
> (...)
>
> In this regard, price fixing and market allocation agreements will be deemed per se illegal when they are not a consequence of nor form part of an integration contract or are not effective to achieve efficiency from such integration. What is intended to explain here is that such agreements jump the per se illegal barrier so their legality must be analysed from the perspective of the "rule of reason."

III. Merger Test

159. The merger test established in Act No. 31112, Merger Control Act, and its Regulations, intends to determine if the transaction under analysis creates a significant restriction to competition on the concerned markets. According to Article 7 of the Merger Control Act, the Antitrust Commission will evaluate the following aspects of the market:

(1) Market structure.
(2) Current or potential competition.
(3) The evolution of supply and demand.
(4) Distribution or commercialization sources.
(5) Legal barriers and other kinds of barriers (technological, horizontal or vertical restrictions) for market entrance.
(6) The economic and financial power of the concerned agents.
(7) The creation or strengthening of a dominant position.
(8) The production of economic efficiencies.

160. For these purposes, the analysis considers productive, allocation or innovative efficiencies that meet the following requirements:

(1) they must be proven by the applicant;
(2) they must be inherent to the concentration;
(3) they must be aimed at outweighing identified restrictive effects on competition stemming from the concentration and improving consumer wellbeing;
(4) they must be transferable to the consumer;
(5) they must be verifiable by the authority.

Chapter 4. Overview of Main Notions

§1. Undertaking

161. Article 2 of the LRCA establishes the subjective application of the LRCA. The rule is applied to all persons and legal entities, irregular societies, autonomous trusts, or other public or private entities with or without profit, which offer or demand goods or services in the market.

162. The law also applies to those who exercise leadership, management or representation of the legal subjects mentioned above, to the extent that they have participated in the planning, implementation, or execution of the administrative offense.

163. Article 2 was modified by Legislative Decree No. 1205 in September 2015 to include in its scope those who are "planners, agents or facilitators" of a per se anticompetitive conduct (i.e., cartels). The amendment states that officers, directors and public servants are included in this category provided that they acted outside their regular functions.

164. Regarding the objective application of the norm, it is important to point out that, according to Article 3, a behavior accepted in a legal provision will not be sanctioned by the LRCA. The respective questioning of the legal rule will be undertaken in the appropriate channel.

§2. Relevant Market

I. How to Define a Relevant Market

165. According to Article 6 of the LRCA, the relevant market must be defined throughout the delimitation of both relevant product market and relevant geographic market.

166. The definition of relevant market is a key element in the evaluation of anticompetitive effects, and its delimitation is required to establish if a firm has market power. This implies evaluating two elements: (i) the relevant product or services market from the point of view of the demand and the supply, and (ii) the relevant geographical market.

167. The identification of the relevant product market aims to establish which set of products are suitable substitutes to each other, i.e., "the set of products that consumers believe are the closest substitutes." If there is a slight but significant non-transitory increase in the price of the set of products selected as relevant, where leading consumers are not opting for third-party products, the relevant product market will be properly defined. The consumer's decision to change the product because of the increase in its price will take into account the characteristics and uses of potential substitutes and the price thereof.

168. For its part, identifying the relevant market equates to defining the geographical area where the alternatives are located to which the economic agent could go if the product's price increases by any amount that is significant and non-transitory. The relevant geographical market can be defined as "the area that includes all the commercial suppliers or commercial locals that consumers consider substitutes of the commercial supplier or commercial local of interest." Defining the relevant geographical market is necessary to evaluate not only the possibilities and limitations that the alternative suppliers face to cater to the buyer but also the ability of the latter to stock up from different suppliers. The analysis of the geographical market's definition focuses on determining the cost to purchase, within the analyzed area, the relevant product from another geographical region, so that the product meets the demand at competitive levels.

169. The key in determining the relevant market is *substitution*. Such substitution can be derived from two dimensions: (i) the substitution on the demand side, and (ii) the substitution on the supply side. The first relates to the increase in the price of a product that makes it less attractive to consumers, so that they decide to buy less of it and more of the substitute product. The second is related to the possibility that, because of a price increase, other suppliers can quickly start offering a substitute product. This type of substitution usually refers to companies that are already making similar products and/or operating in adjacent areas. The difference between this substitution and the entry of new competitors is that the first will require little or no investment.

170. In the case of substitution on the demand side what must be seen is the consumer's response to a price increase. Thus, if the price of product A rises, the consumers react by buying less of that product and more of product B, making product B a substitute for A.

171. To define the relevant market, the authority considers the implementation of the Hypothetical Monopolist Test (HMT). This test consists of defining the market as a product or group of products for which a hypothetical monopolist could impose, in a profitable way, price increases by a slight amount that is significant and non-transitory (also known as Small but Significant Non-Transitory Increase in Price (SSNIP) Test). The iterative process ends when the selected set of products satisfies the test.

172. Complementing the hypothetical monopolist test, the authority often observes other kinds of information to shed some light on the consumer's reaction to a change in price. In the Peruvian case, for example, the competition agency noted, among others, the following information:

(1) Preferences of the customers or consumers.
(2) Characteristics, uses and prices of potential substitutes.

(3) Technological possibilities and the required time for substitution.

173. In short, to determine the relevant market, the competition agency looks for any data that shows how consumers will react to a change in the price of products (substitution by the demand's side).

174. In the case of substitution by the supply side, the competition agency must verify whether a price increase leads to the offering, in the short term, of an effective substitute. The substitution by the supply side will not always be applicable in all relevant market definition cases, making the competition agency responsible for determining if it is necessary to incorporate this dimension in their analysis or if the relevant market will be defined primarily by the substitution on the demand side. In the latter case (when the application is discarded), the authority must support its decision because it could be distorting the analysis.

II. Market Definition in INDECOPI's Decisions

175. In *Group Multipurpose S.R.L. and Dispra E.I.R.L. v. Quimpac S.A. and Clorox Perú S.A*[45], the claimants filed a complaint against the Quimpac and Clorox for abusing their dominant position as they subscribed an exclusive sodium hypochlorite distribution contract that restrained the complainants to continue to act in the bleach production market. The Commission concluded that Quimpac had a dominant position since it held a monopoly in the bleach production and merchandising market. While performing its analysis, the Commission detected that the relevant market was constituted only by sodium hypochlorite produced in Peru, since importation would not be financially profitable and there were no substitute products.

176. In *Aeroservicios S.A.C. v. PETROPERU*[46], the complainant affirmed that PETROPERU had a dominant position in the Turbo A-1 fuel sale in the wholesale market. The Commission considered there was not a substitute product for the Turbo A-1, because it was the only fuel used by commercial aviation. Furthermore, it pointed out that the geographical market would be formed by the department of Piura, since a "small but significant and not transitory" price increase in the Talara Refinery would not make the product buyers move to other areas.

177. In *Termochilca S.A.C. v. The members of ConsorcioCamisea*[47], the first one claimed that the second ones were abusing their dominant position in the natural gas market. Even though the parties reached a transaction, the Commission continued the procedure and established that the relevant market was the natural gas from Camisea, which could not be substituted by other fuels due to the different prices, or by the production of other areas in Peru because the facilities to take that gas to

45. Resolution No. 005-2008-CLC-INDECOPI.
46. Resolution No. 009-2010/CLC-INDECOPI.
47. Resolution No. 054-2010/CLC-INDECOPI.

the zone where Termochilca would build its plant (Chilca) do not exist. Therefore, given there are not any alternative sources of supply in the area, it was concluded that the only possible provider were the defendants. Thus, the Commission identified that there was a dominant position, even if it later determined that there was not any abuse.

178. In *Metales Bera del Peru S.A. v. Minsur S.A.*,[48] which is perhaps the most influential precedent about relevant market definition in Peru, Bera accused Minsur of refusing to sell tin concentrates. INDECOPI established that tin importation is not subject to any administrative barrier and has a 15% tax, except for the Bolivian importations, which have a 0% tax, due to Decision 321 of the Cartagena Agreement. Likewise, Minsur's mine is in the Department of Puno, near Bolivia, so there were no important transportation costs. This led the Commission to consider Peru and Bolivia as the relevant market.[49,50]

179. In the case, INDECOPI established that it was necessary to relate the market share to the ability to determine the price. If other area's suppliers can provide the same or similar products or services in the claimant's influence area, or if consumers turn to other options, INDECOPI considers them as substitutes. What is important is to establish a relation between the idea of a dominant position and the ability to affect the price, in other words, of not being a "price taker."

§3. Market Power/Dominant Position

I. General Discussion

180. Once the relevant competitors are recognized, it is possible to determine the market share of an agent. Usually in Peru, the calculation to get the market share utilizes sales as the main variable; however, in cases in which there is price differentiation among companies or high volatility, the volume of production or the company's patrimony can also be used. Nevertheless, market share alone is not enough to conclude on market power.

181. There can be companies with a big presence on the market that do not have market power, or companies with a market share of only 35% that are able to put

48. Resolution No. 066-96-INDECOPI/CLC.

49. While with the definition of Peru as the relevant market, Minsur practically had a monopoly, the definition of Peru and Bolivia as a relevant market reduced Minsur's participation to 46%.

50. Resolution No. 117-97-TDC. In this decision, the Tribunal noticed the following: "(…) Of the documentation appearing in the file such as the information provided by Minsur, it's inferred that Minsur has a 46% participation percentage in the tin market in Peru and Bolivia. This percentage is lower than half of amount of tin produced in the relevant market and the Chamber agreed with the Commission criteria in the sense that it doesn't allow it to have a dominant position. Therefore, even if we considered Peru and Bolivia as the relevant market, which is the most beneficial situacion for Bera's position, as it excludes the other possible competitors, Minsur doesn't hold a dominant position. (…)."

pressure over prices. Factors such as a high elasticity of demand or low barriers of entry to the market cut the market power of any company. On the other hand, a market with few substitutes, legal barriers or high capital requirements will boost and reinforce the dominant position of a company with a high market share. Still, market share has been regularly used in Peruvian cases of competition as an indicator of market power, especially when it stays high over a long period of time.

182. In the determination of market power, the analysis of homogenous products is usually not enough. Substitutes of roughly similar prices must also be considered within the relevant market, as they impose an important limitation to the power of any company. Price elasticity must be complemented with cross elasticity of other products to determine real market power in the case of monopolies.

183. Once the market is delimited, the authority must use indicators to calculate market power. As said before, the market share is a common indicator. However, a better indicator is the Herfindahl-Hirschman Index (HHI). This indicator shows the market concentration, which helps to determine whether a company has the capacity to alter prices. The index is calculated as follows:

$$H = \sum_{i=1}^{N} r_i^2$$

In the formula, r_i represents the market share of company i and N represents the number of companies. In the U.S.A., a level of H higher than 0.18 reflects a concentrated market, in which leaders have the ability to control prices.

II. INDECOPI's Decisions about Market Power

184. HHI is used by INDECOPI as referential but not as the only criteria for determining market power. For example, in *Aldem S.A.C. contra TalmaMenzies S.R.L.*[51] it was determined that the defendant did not hold a dominant position, since even though it had more than a 50% market share, it encountered an intense actual and potential competition, considering that Swissport and Shohin had a joint participation of more than 40%.

185. In *Bera v. Minsur,*[52] the Commission considered that 47% of the relevant market (tin produced in Peru and Bolivia) did not constitute a dominant position in favor of the accused.

51. Resolution No. 002-2005-INDECOPI/CLC.
52. Resolution No. 066-96-INDECOPI/CLC.

186. Similarly, in the Asociación Editorial Bruño v. Other members of the Comité de Fabricantes de Material Didáctico de la Sociedad Nacional de Industrias[53], it was considered that a dominant position did not exist since defendant's market share was 50%.

187. In *EmpresaEditora El Comercio S.A. v. Aero Continente S.A.,*[54] both Tribunal and Commission considered that Aero Continente held a dominant position only in the Lima-Iquitos, Lima-Pucallpa, Lima-Puerto Maldonado and Lima-Tarapoto routes, as it was the only company that covered them, and not in other routes in which it competed with other companies.

188. Even though an express precedent has not been established, INDECOPI's practice shows that the turning point between the existence or not of the dominant position revolves around a market participation of 50%, which is similar to the criteria developed in the European system.

§4. Agreements and Concerted Practices

189. Competition policy and the prohibition of concerted practices have been enforced in Peru for less than thirty years. Before 1991, the State itself promoted these practices. The government used to summon the main suppliers of certain consumer goods to settle a price that was "adequate" for them. By doing this, they kept the consumers from their right to influence on prices. Furthermore, meetings that took place were considered the righteous way to operate. So much so that such agreements were often considered a "gentlemen's pact."

190. The State was a victim of this culture of agreements. In tenders, companies agreed upon the bids they would make, and this caused great inefficiencies for the consumers of the services or products in the bidding process. Upon the creation of INDECOPI, some markets were so used to agreeing on prices that they did not consider it to be wrong. Thus, many illegal practices were not caused by a desire to break the law but by the maintenance of the status quo.

191. Agreements to settle prices at a determined level bring a reduction in the level of production. In this idea rests the criticism of concerted practices. The level of production will be below the social equilibrium, so not only will some buyers be forced to pay more; most importantly, there will be a group of consumers that will not be able to purchase anymore. The condemning ideas toward price agreements rely on the defense of these consumers, as they can no longer buy the goods that they bought before due to the expropriation of their rights to take part in the price formation.

---

53. Resolution No. 067-96-INDECOPI/CLC.
54. Resolution No. 0078-1999/TDC-INDECOPI.

192. As said, cartels have difficulties to last over long periods of time. There are two main issues surrounding cartels that would obstruct their price settlements:

(1) Maintaining prices artificially high creates an important incentive for possible competitors to start operating on the market. A positive mark-up, which is held despite any movement in demand, attracts many investors as the risk is much less. The entrance of these companies will undermine the cartel's power, generating a downside pressure over prices. In the end, as long as the mark-up stays positive, new companies will be interested to enter the market. This will continue until the artificial price is corrected. Obviously, this corrective mechanism requires low barriers of entry.
(2) Member companies of the cartel will also be tempted to "betray" the cartel. Their incentives to betray will depend on several factors, including their market share, the level of extraordinary benefits generated by the cartel and, since the agreement is dynamic, the interest rate.

193. Agreements and concerted practices have an important difference in the accumulation of market power. The objective of any company is to gain market share through the implementation of better practices and increasing efficiencies. This willingness to improve has obvious benefits, so the prohibition to concentrate power will have negative effects on the economy. Cartels, however, do not increase efficiencies and do not generate improvements for consumers. For these reasons, there is room for regulation in these cases, at least more so than in cases of the presence of dominant positions.

§5. Restriction of Competition

194. The most common practices to restrict competition are access restraints, tying, exclusivity agreements and predatory prices. Some of these have anticompetitive results and can have a negative effect on the consumers under certain circumstances.

195. Under the threat of companies entering the market, leading companies can assume different strategies. These strategies will depend on several aspects, such as the market structure, the size of the new competitor, the expectations of the industry, etc. For example, if a company is about to enter the market pointing at a sector that was previously unattended by the incumbent, the incumbent will have to make a choice. It can either block the entrance by creating a brand that attacks that segment or let the new company enter, and just concentrate in not losing its current costumers.

196. For a restriction of competition to happen, the agent must behave against the basic principles typified in the LRCA. This does not necessarily imply that there must be an intention to distort the competitive process. It is enough to determine if the conduct is objectively disloyal and has a negative impact on the market. Only if we are analyzing predatory practices, the intentionality must be proved.

§6. Abuse of Dominance

197. The Peruvian Constitution states in Article 61 that: "The State facilitates and oversees free competition. It fights any practice that would limit it and the abuse of dominant or monopolistic positions. No law or arrangement may authorize or establish monopolies."

198. As can be seen, having a dominant position is not prohibited. However, dominant firms must follow certain rules and parameters to avoid harming competition because of their conducts.

199. An "illegal abuse of dominance" must be understood as the use of dominant power to cause exclusionary effects. Damages derived from a free and fair competition through price, quality and condition commercialization cannot be sanctioned. This is perhaps the main problem with the abuse of dominant position. How to differentiate the exclusionary effects from the consequences of a regular competition? Both can be very similar: reduction of participation of competitors in this market.

200. The use of market power can be understood in two ways, depending on the circumstances. The first is the use of the efficiencies derived from economies of scale. In fact, companies develop competitive capabilities based on their size. This allows them to reduce costs, integrate its operations, and thus offer better products at better prices. The second is that the size gives the possibility of obtaining illicit benefits that could not have been obtained other way.

201. If the authority penalizes a company for using its productive efficiency to compete, then it is penalizing precisely the market efficiency that this company generates. In doing so the message sent is that companies should not be too efficient. This situation requires cautious actions from the authority. It follows that the legality of the practice must be presumed, if there is any doubt of its illegal nature. The harmful, exclusionary effects must have been accredited sufficiently and the potential benefits of the conduct must not be important enough. Only if that occurs, the conduct can be finally qualified as an abuse of dominance.

202. Therefore, a conduct will be sanctioned *ex post* only if it has exclusionary effects. The abuse of dominance with exploitative effects is not considered illegal in Peru, since this behavior usually causes the entry of new competitors attracted by the profits of the dominant. A clear example of this is the "excessive" price for a particular good or service.

§7. Concentrations

203. The new Merger Control Act defines concentration operations as any act or operation that involves a transfer or change in control of a company or part of it. The term "permanent" has been removed from the definition of a concentration act in the new law. Nonetheless, considering the regulations, the change of control should be intended to be permanent for an operation to qualify as a concentration.

204. "Control" is defined as the possibility of exerting a decisive and continuous influence over an economic agent through rights of ownership or use of all or part of a company's assets, or rights or contracts that allow a decisive and continuous influence on the structure, deliberations, or decisions of a company's bodies, determining, either directly or indirectly, the competitive strategy of a firm.

205. Considering this, Law No. 31112 and its complementary regulations state that concentrations within the scope of the law can arise because of:

(1) a merger;
(2) the conclusion of an associative contract or joint venture which results in the creation of an economic agent which is intended to be permanent and fully functional;
(3) the direct or indirect acquisition of control over other companies through different means, such as the acquisition of shares, participations, or through any other contract or legal figure that confers direct or indirect control of a company; and
(4) the acquisition of productive assets (i) to which a defined income volume is attributable; (ii) that can reinforce or increase the market share of the acquirer; and (iii) that have generated income during the year prior to notification.

§8. Joint Ventures

206. Joint ventures are subject to *ex ante* merger control only if the transaction grants the participating parties direct or indirect control over another company participating in the relevant market.

207. According to Act No. 31112, joint ventures are subject to merger control if they result in the acquisition of joint control over one or more economic agents. Particularly the act refers to the establishment by two or more economic agents of a joint undertaking, joint venture or any other similar contractual arrangement that entails the acquisition of joint control over one or more economic agents, in such a way as to permanently perform the functions of an autonomous economic entity in the market.

Chapter 5. Consequences of Violations and Enforcement Institutions

§1. Administrative Enforcement

208. The main cause of action against the breach of antitrust rules is administrative proceedings handled by the Commission. The goal of the proceedings is to determine administrative liability by declaring the existence of a breach (or not) to antitrust rules and imposing administrative sanctions, when pertinent.

209. These proceedings are not of a private nature and do not aim to repair private parties from antitrust damage. The Commission cannot address private claims and the proceedings do not aim specifically to address a private party's claim.

210. INDECOPI and their Commissions were created in large part to provide an alternative to Peruvian courts, which had proven to be inefficient in these matters due to overload of cases and lack of specialization. The Commissions have been granted quasi-judicial powers to prosecute, investigate, and declare anticompetitive practices.

I. The Antitrust Authorities

211. As we have explained lines above, competition law and policy was formally introduced to Peru in 1991 with the enactment of Legislative Decree No. 701 and consolidated in 1993 with the opening of INDECOPI, a governmental agency with technical, administrative, economic, and budgetary autonomy, which enforces both the laws and regulations that promote competition and protecting intellectual property. Legislative Decree No. 701 was in force until June 2008, when the government enacted the LRCA.

A. *Formation; Composition*

212. In Peru, the application of the LRCA is under the exclusive jurisdiction of an administrative agency: INDECOPI.[55] INDECOPI is responsible for handling the

55. Legislative Decree No. 1033.—Legislative Decree approving the Law on the Organization and Functions of the National Institute for Defense of Competition and Protection of Intellectual Property – INDECOPI:

> Article 2°.—INDECOPI functions
> 2.1 INDECOPI is the autonomous agency in charge of:
> (…)
>
> b) Safeguard free and fair competition and punish unfair competitive behavior in order to ensure effective competition in the market (…).

administrative procedure for the violation of the LRCA, in both claims and ex officio cases.[56] The Antitrust Commission is formed by four members, who are generally lawyers and economists. They are appointed by INDECOPI's Board for a period of five years.[57] Likewise, INDECOPI's Board consists of five members, appointed by the President of the Council of Ministers for a period of five years. The President of INDECOPI's Board is appointed for the same period by the President of Peru.[58]

213. The NDC is the technical autonomous agency or entity which instructs the investigation and sanctioning procedure, presenting the case and issuing its opinion on the existence of the anticompetitive conduct.

214. It is worth mentioning that the Commission will act in the proceedings filed for violation of the competition rules as the first administrative instance. In that line, its decisions could be reviewed by INDECOPI's Defense of Competition Tribunal[59] that acts as the second and final administrative instance on the matter.

215. The only possible recourse against the last instance decisions of INDECOPI's Defense of Competition Tribunal is the judicial review through the so-called administrative litigation proceedings.[60]

---

56. Legislative Decree No. 1033:

> Article 24°.—Antitrust Commission.—
> Antitrust Commission safeguards observance of the Law Against Monopolistic, Controller and Restrictive Practices Affecting Competition, Anti-monopolistic and Anti-oligopolistic Law of the Electric Sector and other laws that prohibit and punish the anticompetitive behaviour or promote an effective competition, as well as those that complements or replace the former laws.

57. Articles 21 and 22 of Legislative Decree No. 1033.
58. Articles 4, 6 and 7 of Legislative Decree No. 1033.
59. Legislative Decree No. 1033:

> Article 14°.—Tribunal Chambers functions.—
> 14.1 The chambers of the Tribunal have the following functions:
>
> a) To know and resolve in second and final administrative instance the appeals filed against such acts that put an end to the case, cause defenselessness or determine the impossibility to continue the proceeding initiated by Commissions, Technical Secretaries or Directors of the Intellectual Property, as the case may be. In that line, they may know about fines imposition for administrative violations or comminatory fines for non-compliance with final resolutions, precautionary, preventive or corrective measures, conciliation agreements and payment of cost and expenses; as well as orders dictated and the adoption of precautionary, corrective or complementary measures.

60. Legislative Decree No. 1033:

> Article 18°.—Exhaustion of the Administrative Remedies and judicial appeal of INDECOP rulings.—

216. In this line, the Peruvian legal system has clearly stated that INDECOPI has exclusive powers to enforce the LRCA. Therefore, the judiciary may review the decisions adopted by INDECOPI but does not have primary jurisdiction to rule upon the matter. That is, the judiciary may only know the case to the extent it is requested to review a previous decision of INDECOPI.

B. Investigating Powers

217. The NDC has the following powers within the preliminary investigation:

(1) Demand individuals, business associations and autonomous properties to exhibit all kinds of documents, including accounting and corporate books, payment vouchers, internal and external correspondence and electronic or magnetic records, including the software required for reading the information; as well as to request information regarding the organization, its businesses, the shareholders and the ownership structure of firms.
(2) Summon or examine, through the officers assigned for such purpose, the individuals under investigation or their representatives, employees, officers, advisors and third parties, using technical resources it deems necessary to generate a complete and accurate record of their statements, being entitled to use magnetic tape recordings in video, compact disc or any other electronic instrument.
(3) To conduct dawn raids, with or without prior notification, at the premises of the natural or legal person, business associations and autonomous properties, and examine books, records, documents and goods, being entitled to check on the development of the production processes and take the statement of the persons found at the premise. In the dawn raid may take copies of physical files, magnetic or electronic, as well as any document that is deemed relevant or taking photographs or filming as may be necessary.
(4) To request judicial authorization to lift the privacy of correspondence and secrecy of telecommunications in order to gather evidence of an infraction.

218. The NDC shall obtain prior judicial authorization to proceed with the forcible unlocking in case any opposition to entry into the premises occur or they were closed, as well as to copy private correspondence that may be contained in physical files or electronic records.

18.1 In those cases under the competence of any decision-making entities or agencies of INDECOPI, the case may be appealed before the Judiciary only when the administrative instances have been exhausted. It is understood, pursuant to this law, that the administrative instance is exhausted when the respective Chamber of the Tribunal for Defense of Competition and Intellectual Protection has issued the final resolution.

C. Adjudicating Powers (Ascertaining and Sanctioning)

219. In accordance with Article 30 of the LRCA, the NDC is entitled, due to its jurisdiction, to perform at its own initiative the necessary proceedings for evidentiary examination of the facts, gathering documents, information or relevant material to determine, as appropriate, whether or not the charged administrative infringement exists.

220. If, following the instruction of the procedure, the initial determination of the facts or its possible description is modified, the NDC will issue a new charging resolution which will replace the decision to initiate the procedure with a list of charges, by informing it to the Commission and notifying the accused persons, as well as the persons who have filed the complaint, if applicable. In case this new decision is issued, a new calculation of deadlines for the formulation of the discharges and a new calculation of the legal period that corresponds to the process proceedings are initiated.

221. In a period no later than thirty working days from the expiration of the probationary period, the NDC will issue a Technical Report indicating the following:

(1) Proven facts.
(2) Determination of the administrative infringement.
(3) Identification of the responsible party.
(4) Proposal for the penalty grading.
(5) Proposal of relevant corrective measures.

222. If the NDC does not find evidence of the existence of anticompetitive conduct, it shall propose to the Commission the declaration of nonexistence of the administrative infringement.

223. The Technical Report shall be notified to the parties in the procedure who will have fifteen working days to make allegations and submit a writing request to speak before the Commission.

224. Once the deadline to submit allegations has expired, the NDC shall have a period of five working days to inform the Commission acted in the procedure, its Technical Report, the arguments of the parties on the Technical Report and, be the case, requests for hearing that had been presented.

225. Once the Commission is informed about the Technical Report and the allegations, it may, in accordance with the requests made by the parties or ex officio, summon the parties to a hearing, considering the need for such diligence to secure sufficient evidence to solve the case, with no less than five days in advance.

226. Exceptionally, the Commission may request the submission of additional evidence, if it considers it relevant to the case. If the Commission orders the submission of additional evidence, the parties shall be entitled to present their own evidence, opening an additional evidentiary phase of thirty working days, which shall be notified to all the parties in the procedure. At the end of this phase, the Commission will have thirty working days to issue its decision.

227. The decision of the Commission shall be substantiated and shall decide over all issues arising from the file. In the decision, the involved parties cannot be ascribed to facts that have not been duly charged during the procedure instruction.

228. The Commission's final decision may be appealed by the defendant party, who has filed the complaint and by third parties with a legitimate interest who have attended to the procedure before the Tribunal within fifteen working days. The NDC may appeal the decision to exonerate the investigated parties, as well as to question the fines imposed.

229. The following acts of the NDC or the Commission can also be subject to an appeal in the same period, as appropriate:

(a) The acts determining the impossibility to continue with the procedure.
(b) Acts that can produce helplessness or irreparable damage to rights or legitimate interests.

D. Other Institutional Tasks (Consultancy to Parliament/Government)

230. According to Article 14 of the LRCA, the Commission is tasked with issuing non-binding guidelines that orientate market agents in all issues involving the correct application and interpretation of the LRCA. Likewise, under the same article, the Commission is tasked with providing public entities with suggestions or recommendations, as well as issuing exhortations, involving actions needed to restore and/or promote competition, such as the elimination of bureaucratic burdens to competition or the application of regulation provided competition is not possible, among others. INDECOPI's Board will submit said recommendations or exhortations to the corresponding entities, which will be required to answer within ninety working days. Both the President of the Council of Ministers and the Ministry of Economy and Finances will also be notified of the above.[61]

61. According to the amendments introduced to Art. 14 by Legislative Decree No. 1205 of September 2015.

II. Government Direct Enforcement Activities

231. In Peru, the application of the LRCA is under the exclusive jurisdiction of INDECOPI[62] and OSIPTEL (in Telecom market). In no event, judiciary shall be appealed without first exhausting the administrative instances before the above-mentioned agencies. The aforesaid implies that other government agencies do not have the authority to do or promote activities related to antitrust law enforcement.

232. Nonetheless, other Peruvian authorities can require INDECOPI's opinion on the legality of certain activities regarding their sectors, as well as recommending INDECOPI to investigate markets and conducts. The decision about initiating an investigation is taken by the Technical Secretariat.

233. Likewise, when the Court of State Contracting identify any conduct that would constitute an anticompetitive practice in terms of this law, it shall communicate such fact to INDECOPI, in order that it, through its competent agents and, if appropriate, initiate an infringement procedure and determine the responsibility that may exist. Only if INDECOPI determines the existence of an offense and it becomes final, the State Contracting Supervisor Agency (OSCE) will proceed to register the offenders in the registry of disqualified suppliers to be contracted by the government.

III. Other Administrative Agencies Applying Antitrust Rules

234. The application of the LRCA in the telecommunication market will be enforced by OSIPTEL (Agency for the Supervision of Private Investment in Telecommunications), according to the authority's functions and powers under Law No. 27336. No other administrative agency enforces antitrust rules directly.

IV. Administrative Fines

235. Anticompetitive practices shall be sanctioned by the Commission based on the Applicable UIT,[63]with the following fines:

---

62. Legislative Decree No. 1033.—Legislative Decree approving the Law on the Organization and Functions of the National Institute for Defence of Competition and Protection of Intellectual Property – INDECOPI:

    Article 2°.—INDECOPI's functions
    2.1. INDECOPI is the autonomous agency in charge of:
    (…)

    b) Safeguard free and fair competition and punish unfair competitive behavior in order to ensure effective competition in the market (…).

63. For 2021, one UIT represents PEN 4,400.00 or USD 1,073.00, approximately.

(1) In case of a minor violation, the fine shall be up to 500 UIT (approx. USD 536,000) with an upper limit of 8% of the sales or gross income of the offender, or its economic group, with regard to all its economic activities during the fiscal year immediately preceding the issuance of the decision of the Commission.
(2) In case of a major violation, the fine shall be up to 1,000 UIT (approx. USD 1.07 million) with an upper limit of 10% of the sales or gross income earned by the offender, or its economic group, with regard to all its economic activities during the fiscal year immediately preceding the issuance of the decision of the Commission.
(3) In case of a serious violation, the upper limit will be 12% of the sales or gross income earned by the offender, or its economic group, with regard to all its economic activities during the fiscal year immediately preceding the issuance of the decision of the Commission.

236. In case of professional or business associations, or economic agents who have started their operations after January 1 of the preceding fiscal year, the fine shall not exceed, in any case, 1,000 UIT.

237. In addition to the fine imposed on offending undertakings, a fine of up to 100 UIT (approx. USD 107,000) may be imposed on officers and legal representatives of the offending undertakings, provided they are responsible for the planning, implementation or execution of the anticompetitive practice.

238. It must be noted that the Commission has the power to terminate procedures early, reduce said fines or even exonerate them, if those involved in the infringement to competition law apply for the benefit mechanisms set forth in Articles 25 and 26 of the LRCA, i.e., the commitment to cease, the leniency benefit and the acknowledgment commitment (Article 26-A).[64]

239. According to Article 25, within the period of forty-five working days from the date of notification of the charges or decision of initiation of the procedure, any of the parties under investigation may request early termination of the procedure in exchange for voluntary corrective measures aimed at ending the alleged infringement, restoring competition, and reversing any negative effects derived from the infringement. In addition to the former, the applicant may offer complementary measures that evidence its purpose of amendment and contribute to the activities of investigation, promotion and defense of competition, including the financial and any other kind of support of said activities.[65]

240. This offering/application will be assessed by the NDC within sixty working days, after which it will propose to the Commission the approval of the applicant's commitment, suggesting applicable compliance measures and a timeframe for

64. According to the amendments introduced by Legislative Decree No. 1205 in September 2015.
65. According to the amendments introduced by Legislative Decree No. 1396 in September 2018.

supervision. The Commission will decide within thirty working days. Due to its discretionary nature, this decision cannot be appealed. Once the timeframe for supervision has expired and the voluntary measures to restore competition have been taken, the Commission will issue a decision acknowledging the above. The benefit does not eliminate or limit civil responsibility for damages derived from the infringement.

241. Failure to comply with this commitment by the applicant will be sanctioned with up to 1,000 UIT, provided that said fine does not exceed 10% of the applicant's or its economic group's gross income for the previous year.

242. On the other hand, Article 26 establishes the leniency benefit (exoneration from sanction), which requires applicants to come forward to the NDC and provide evidence that helps detect or prove the existence of an anticompetitive collusion practice (*hard-core cartels*). Article 26.2 establishes a series of procedural regulations involving the application, for example, timeframes to submit incriminating evidence that applicants will be expected to comply within their duty as collaborators.

243. Once the NDC considers that the applicant has provided sufficient evidence to support initiating an ex officio administrative procedure against those involved in the infringement to the LRCA, it will negotiate signing a leniency agreement, which establishes the scope of collaboration expected from the applicant and the confidential nature of its participation in the agreement.

244. Unless the NDC informs the Commission of a confirmed breach in the applicant's duty as a collaborator and that this breach has not been rectified by the applicant after a reasonable period after being informed of it, the Commission will grant the benefit, which is enforceable against any other administrative entity. However, the Commission will deny the benefit if the applicant is found to have exert coercion in other cartel members to join the cartel. The latter will only be eligible to apply for a reduction of fines.

245. Likewise, in the case of several applicants, only the first that has provided evidence of the existence of an anticompetitive conduct and the identity of the offenders will benefit from the exoneration. Other economic agents that provide relevant information may be benefited with the reduction of the fine, if that information is different from the one that the competition authority already has, either by own research or because of the first applicant's collaboration. Second applicants may be granted a reduction of fines between 30% and 50%, whereas third applicants may be granted a reduction of 20% to 30%. Subsequent applicants may be granted a reduction of up to 20%.

246. Applications for the leniency benefit filed once the procedure has begun will only be considered if the evidence voluntarily put forth by the applicants has a significantly added value to the investigation and the procedure than that already in the hands of the NDC. If this were the case, the late applicant will be eligible for a reduction of fines benefit.

247. It must be noted that receiving the leniency benefit does not exempt the applicants from civil liability, if any.

248. Finally, Article 26-A establishes the possibility any party under investigation for an alleged anticompetitive infringement has of acknowledging its involvement in said conduct and accepting its responsibility for it. In exchange, the applicant will receive a 15% reduction of the applicable fine. This benefit is lost if the said applicant appeals the Commission's decision to impose a fine.

V. Administrative Injunctions and Other Restrictive Orders

249. In addition to the fines that the Commission could impose for the infringement of the LRCA, it may order corrective measures to restore the competitive process. Article 46 of the LRCA establishes a non-restricted list of measures that can be ordered by the authority:

(1) The suspension or the execution of activities, even under specific conditions.
(2) According to the circumstances, the obligation to contract, even under specific conditions.
(3) The unenforceability of the anticompetitive clauses or provisions of legal acts.
(4) The access to an intermediary association or organization.
(5) The implementation of training and compliance programs aimed at eliminating the risks of a breach of competition law.[66]

VI. Interim Measures

250. According to Article 23 of the LRCA, the Commission has the faculty to order, before the initiation of infringement procedure or at any stage in it, upon request of the NDC, complainant or a third party having legitimate interest, interim measures to ensure the efficacy of the final decision, which includes ensuring the execution of the correctives measures that may be ordered.

251. These measures could be innovative or noninnovative, generic or specific. Particularly, the Commission can order the cessation of activities, obligate parties to contract, impose contract conditions, suspend the effects of legal acts, force parties to adopt positives conducts, and any other measures contributing to preserve the affected competence and avoid the damage that such conducts may generate to the

66. According to the amendments introduced by Legislative Decree No. 1396 in September 2018.

procedure. It is important that the interim measures consider the intensity, proportion and need of the damages to avoid. At any stage during the procedure, the suspension, amendment or revocation of interim measures may be agreed.

252. When precautionary measure is granted before the initiation of an infringement procedure, such measure shall expire if such infringement procedure is not initiated within fifteen working days from its notification.

253. The LRCA also establishes that in case of petitions by one of the parties, the Commission may accept or reject them in a period no more than thirty working days, extendable just once and for the same period. The applicant is not required to provide civil assuring measures such as bonds, counter-measures or any other of similar nature. The Commission may grant different interim measures from those requested, if these correspond to the intensity, proportion and need of the damage to avoid.

254. The Commission's decisions imposing interim measures are appealable before the Tribunal in a period of fifteen working days.[67] The appeal of precautionary measures shall be granted without suspension of its effects. The Tribunal shall state the appeal within a period not exceeding thirty working days. The Tribunal has the same attributions as the Commission to order interim measures.

255. It is important to point out that according to Article 24 of the LRCA, to order an interim measure, the Commission shall verify the fulfillment of the following concurrent requirements:

(1) The payment of the procedural right fee amounting to a half tax reference unit.
(2) The verisimilitude of the complaint.
(3) The danger of final decision delay.
(4) The possibility of granting the requested.

§2. Civil Enforcement

I. Competent Civil Courts

256. Follow-on claims on damages are handled by civil courts. These cases follow the same private damages rules as any torts or contractual liability matter and are thus governed by civil liability procedural rules and jurisdiction. Cases are decided by the civil courts in the first instance (whose jurisdiction varies according to the defendant's domicile and the amount in dispute), by the Courts of Appeals in the second instance and, exceptionally, by the Peruvian Supreme Court (if cassation is granted).

67. Based on the application of Law No. 27444.

II. Sanctions

A. *Nullity*

257. The courts have power to declare an agreement or any kind of contract null if the judge considers it is against the law.

B. *Damages*

1. Declarations

258. First of all, it is important to say that the main remedy established by the LRCA is a declarative decision issued by the Commission (and not a Civil Court). In this decision, the Commission declares the admissibility of the complaint and either the existence or not of an anticompetitive conduct (that is, the conduct is unlawful as an infringement to competition law). In the same decision the Commission determines administrative liability and imposes sanctions or corrective measures.

2. Compensatory Damages

259. Under Peruvian law, damages are available as a remedy to anticompetitive conduct.

260. Article 49 of the LRCA provides very little guidance and does not provide specific rules for quantum of damages in antitrust damages actions. Antitrust damages actions are treated as civil liability cases. Civil liability rules and procedures will apply.

261. As a consequence, Peruvian law does not address the complexity that the antitrust damages actions can entail. Significantly, there is no specific regulation as to possible defenses or on how damages shall be assessed or proven or relating to the participation of INDECOPI in these proceedings.

262. As with most civil law countries, in the Peruvian legal framework, damages are mainly treated as a mechanism to compensate the victim and not as a mechanism to deter unlawful actions. Damages are awarded to compensate a particular damage. The principle of full compensation applies, implying that the award must place the victim in a position as close as possible to that in which it would have been had the damage not occurred. Damages must be limited to compensate for the loss actually suffered (*damnumemergens*) and the loss of profits (*lucrumcessans*). There are no punitive damages. In very limited cases, moral damages to individuals are admitted as part of the compensation. There is no rule establishing restrictions for recoverable amounts on damages other than demanding that said damages are proven and have adequate causation with the anticompetitive behavior.

263. Infringement of antitrust provisions can give rise to a tort claim.

264. Article 49 of the LRCA provides a statutory basis for the recovery of damages relating to antitrust actions. Article 49 of the LRCA sets forth the victim's right to claim compensation for economic damages resulting from anticompetitive behavior and establishes the cause of action. According to such article, once the administrative proceedings brought before INDECOPI (or OSIPTEL) are concluded, any person who has been injured by a breach of antitrust rules can claim damages under the civil liability rules before civil courts, provided they are able to prove . Thus, tort is a cause of action for the recovery of antitrust damages provided that the administrative proceedings before INDECOPI have been exhausted only following a prior infringement decision.

265. With a prior favorable opinion of the NDC, the Commission is entitled to initiate a civil claim in defense of the diffuse and collective interest of affected consumers for alleged damages resulting from anticompetitive practices.[68]

266. In the development of the LRCA, the Guidelines on Compensation for Damages Caused to Consumers as a Result of Anticompetitive Conducts (hereinafter, "the Guidelines on Damage Compensation") establish the terms, rules, conditions or restrictions necessary for the exercise of this action.

267. For instance, the Guidelines determine the types of consumers that should be taken into consideration when determining the scope of the action. This can be classified into two groups: (i) direct buyer, as a natural or legal person who has directly acquired from an infringer products or services that were the subject of an infringement of the LRCA; and (ii) diffuse and collective interests, as those that belong to an indeterminate set of consumers (diffuse interests), or a determined or determinable (collective interest) set of consumers that are linked to each other and that can be grouped within the same class, to determine the damage by an anticompetitive conduct.

268. To establish tort, a claimant must show statutory infringement, the damage suffered or loss and causation. Statutory infringement must be proved by INDECOPI's decision, which is binding as to this matter.

269. Several obstacles make it difficult for victims to recover damages arising out of anticompetitive conduct.

270. First, the LRCA provides INDECOPI and OSIPTEL with original and exclusive jurisdiction to determine the breach of antitrust rules (First Complementary Article of the LRCA). The judiciary cannot decide over this matter even if the issue is relevant for a decision on damages. In practice, this means a necessary bifurcation of the proceedings leading to damages recovery.

---

68. According to the amendments introduced by Legislative Decree No. 1396 in September 2018.

271. The failure to join actions in single proceedings to both determine a breach of antitrust rules and compensate the victim or victims for antitrust injury, together with the lack of an appropriate coordination between such proceedings, explains to a great extent the little development that private damage actions have had in Peru.

272. Since damage actions can only be commenced once the administrative decisions are final, the system condemns antitrust victims to wait no less than three to five years before they can initiate an action for damages and to no less than four to six additional years before they can receive some compensation for the damages suffered. The waiting period for the victim can increase significantly if INDECOPI's decision in determining antitrust liability is challenged before the judiciary. In addition, antitrust laws do not provide specific rules to evaluate and assess antitrust damages. Aspects such as causation, burden of proof and quantum are subject to civil liability rules as explained below.

273. The judicial system offers its own set of problems, adding to the poor development of antitrust damages actions. Peru has no real system of judicial precedents and there is little publicity of judicial opinions. Judicial precedents are few and poor, which means decisions lacking consistency and development. Significantly, Peruvian civil courts have no specialization or expertise in antitrust.

274. In practice, all the above determines no enforcement of antitrust damages actions, weakening the competition law enforcement system. There is no record of a successful damages action in the two decades of competition law enforcement in Peru. Moreover, it is unclear how many damages actions have ever been brought since 1991. The effectiveness of the rules for recovering damages stemming from anticompetitive conducts is a crucial issue to be addressed by competition policy in Peru.

275. A serious effort to enhance antitrust damages actions was made by INDECOPI during the drafting of the LRCA where a quasi-mandatory arbitration for damages action was included in the draft version of the law. The proposal also regulated different procedural and substantive aspects of damages claims (reduction of the burden of proof of the victims, participation of competition agencies in the assessment of damages, among others). Unfortunately, the proposal was left aside by the Executive Branch in the final steps of the enactment of the law.

276. Although there is no specific initiative at the moment, it is expected that new proposals will emerge in the short term to strengthen private actions as a mechanism to enforce antitrust laws.

277. As of August 2021, we only have information of three claims filed before the judiciary for civil damages involving anticompetitive practices. The first two involve abuse of dominance cases and specifically a refusal to deal practice, while the third involves a price-fixing cartel in the drugstore market.

278. The first case was dismissed in 2007 since the administrative decision declaring the existence of anticompetitive behavior (Commission's administrative decision) was not final and could therefore be appealed before INDECOPI's Tribunal.[69] Based on public information, there has not been a final decision involving the second case, since the party declared responsible by INDECOPI for the anticompetitive infringement alleges the statute of limitations for the claim has expired. This discussion has been taken to the highest judiciary authority and is still pending.[70] The third case was filed by INDECOPI itself in October 2019 and as to date, there have not been any public developments on the claim.

a. Restitution

279. Under Peruvian civil liability rules, damages are awarded under the principle of full compensation. Therefore, the award of damages does not include disgorgement or account for profits gained illicitly by the engagement in anticompetitive conduct. However, the determination of the sanction to be imposed by INDECOPI to an infringing party shall weigh in elements to guarantee the fulfillment of the purpose of deterrence (Article 44 of the LRCA) such as the expected illicit benefits (profits), market loss by competitors, the nature and scope of the restriction to competition, duration of the anticompetitive conduct, recurrence, between others. Although this is not specifically an account for profits, Article 44 undoubtedly incorporates expected and actual profits into the calculation of sanctions.

b. Punitive, Exemplary, Aggravated or Multiple Damages

280. Under Peruvian law victims are awarded single damages. Punitive, exemplary, aggravated, or multiple damages are not recognized by the civil liability regime in which damages are only awarded to compensate a particular damage, and damages must be limited to compensate the loss suffered. Since no specific rules exist for damages arising out of antitrust actions, these are not available for antitrust victims.

c. Interest

281. The award of interest becomes relevant only in the context of antitrust damages actions, where civil rules will once more apply.

282. Under general civil liability rules, courts can award interest in any debt or damages action. Interests are due to compensate the winning party for default in payment (Article 1242 of the Peruvian Civil Code). When the parties have not

69. Case sanctioned by INDECOPI's Tribunal by Resolution No. 0068-2009/SC1-INDECOPI of February 2009 (*Group Multipurpose E.I.R.L. and DISPRA E.I.R.L. v. QUIMPAC S.A. and CLOROX DEL PERÚ S.A.*).
70. Case sanctioned by OSIPTEL's collegiate body by Resolution No. 52-2002-CCO/OSIPTEL of July 2002 (*AT&T Perú S.A. v. Telefónica del Perú S.A.A.*).

agreed on the interest rate, interest will be determined by applying the legal interest rate. In torts actions, interest will accrue from the date in which the damage was caused (Article 1985 of the Peruvian Civil Code). In all other cases, interest will accrue from the date the creditor gave notice of default to the debtor (Article 1333 of the Peruvian Civil Code). When the amount needs to be settled by a court or tribunal, such as tort cases and among then private antitrust damages actions, notice of default is deemed to have occurred at the date of notice of the filing of the claim to the defendant (Article 1334 of the Peruvian Civil Code).

283. For interest to be awarded by courts, a party must request interest in its claim. This is confirmed by the Guidelines on Damage Compensation. It should be noted that, in compliance with the provisions, the favorable report of the NDC that supports the relevance of promoting the compensation claim must specify the type of damage claimed as well as the compensation amount, including legal interests.

C. *Interim Measures*

284. The courts have power to dictate a broad range of orders as interim injunctions to ensure payments, such as seizures. Interim injunctions may be issued ex officio or at a private party's request, provided that the requesting party participates in the proceedings.

§3. Criminal Enforcement

I. Criminal Sanctions for Antitrust Violations

285. Until 2020, there were no statutory provisions within the Peruvian antitrust or criminal systems for the imposition of criminal sanctions for antitrust violations.

286. However, in August 2020, the Peruvian congress issued Law No. 31040, which amended the Peruvian Penal Code and criminalized the conducts of abuse of economic power, hoarding and price gouging. These modifications were proposed and approved by the Congress during the early months of the COVID-19 pandemic, when the demand for facial masks, oxygen tanks and pharmaceutical products, amidst other COVID-19-related goods, increased significantly.

287. Law No. 31040 reintroduced Article 232 to the Penal Code, which was repealed in 2008 by Legislative Decree No. 1034 (LRCA). This provision establishes a term of imprisonment between two and six years for those who incur in the conduct of abuse of economic power, consisting of "abuse of dominant position and participation in practices and agreements aimed at restricting competition," thus criminalizing the conducts typified in Articles 10, 11 and 12 of the LRCA.

288. Unlike the LRCA, the current Article 232 of the Penal Code carries generic formulas when it comes to define "abuse of a dominant position." As a result, it is unclear whether exploitative conduct that has no exclusionary effects would be considered an "abuse of dominance" and therefore a criminal offense (e.g., excessive pricing).

289. Likewise, in relation to "restrictive practices and agreements," it has not been specified what type of concerted practices or agreements restrictive of competition would be included in the approved classification.

290. In this sense, a broad interpretation of the criminal type in question could include all types of agreements, even those that currently are not considered per se unlawful by the LRCA, such as vertical agreements or ancillary agreements which are not cartels.

II. Other Application of Criminal Law to Relevant Conducts

291. Law No. 31040 also introduced the crime of hoarding and price gouging (Articles 233 and 234 of the Penal Code, respectively). This classification seeks to sanction commercial conduct that could directly or indirectly affect the prices of certain goods or services classified as essential in emergency contexts (e.g., the COVID-19 pandemic). The common element required in both cases is that the conducts (hoarding or price gouging) must be aimed at "altering customary prices" or to increase "the prices of essential customary goods and services."

292. In this sense, its configuration should require a constitutional emergency declaration and the publication of a list of essential goods and services. Based on a systematic reading of the law and its Final Complementary Provision, no administrative or judicial instance should apply these figures if the declaration of emergency by the President is not previously verified and, subsequently, the publication of a list of assets and essential services. As of the date, this has not happened yet.

III. Role of Prosecutors

293. So far it is not clear whether, for the application of the articles of the Criminal Code that regulate the crimes of abuse of dominance, hoarding and price gouging, it is necessary to exhaust the administrative route before resorting to the judiciary. Although Law No. 31040 does not clarify this matter, the initiation of a criminal action for crimes related to matters within the competence of INDECOPI should not be constitutionally valid, without a prior ruling from the said administrative authority. The determination of an infringement of the LRCA requires technical expertise by INDECOPI.

294. According to Article 18 of Legislative Decree No. 1033, in matters within the competence of INDECOPI, the judiciary may not be resorted to until the administrative procedure has been previously exhausted, which implies that a final decision by the administrative instances of INDECOPI must be obtained prior to the initiation of a criminal case.

IV. Competent Criminal Courts

295. According to the Criminal Procedural Code—Legislative Decree No. 957, the competent court is the one in the territory where the crime was committed. Given that the competence of the Collegiate Criminal Courts is reserved for those matters provided by law, and that Law No. 31040 does not establish any special rule applicable neither to the crime of abuse of economic power nor to the crimes of hoarding or price gouging, the competent court to decide over said crimes would be the Unipersonal Criminal Court of the territory where the crime was committed.

Part II. The Application of the Prohibitions

Chapter 1. Restrictive Agreements

§1. Horizontal Agreements

I. Cartels

296. The so-called restrictive practices or cartels are agreements, decisions, collective recommendations or concerted practices used by different companies operating in the same level of production or distribution of goods and services for the purpose of limiting competition in the whole or part of the market in which such agents participate.

297. In Peru, "horizontal collusive practices" are prohibited by Article 11 of the LRCA.[71] The referred article states that "Horizontal Collusive practices" "are concerted agreements, decisions, recommendations or concerted practices between competitors that have the object or effect of restricting, preventing or distorting competition … ."

---

71. LRCA:

> Article 11.—Horizontal Collusive Practices.—
>
> 11.1. Horizontal collusive practices are those agreements, decisions, recommendations or concerted practices carried out by economic agents' competitors among them, with the purpose or effect of restrict, prevent or distort the competition, such as:
>
> (a) To fix, direct or indirectly, prices or other business or service conditions.
> (b) To limit or control the production, distribution, technical development or investments.
> (c) To distribute concertedly customers, suppliers or geographical zones.
> (d) To agree the product quality, when it is not in accordance to national or international technical standards and adversely affects the consumers.
> (e) To apply in business relations or services, concerted different conditions for equivalent services positioning, without justification, certain competitors in an unfavorable condition with respect to others.
> (f) To subject, concertedly and without justification, the entering into contracts upon acceptance of complementary services that, by their nature or in accordance with the business rules, are not consistent with the purpose of such contracts.
> (g) To deny, concertedly and without justification, to satisfy the selling or acquisition, or to accept selling or rendering offers of goods and services respectively.
> (h) To prevent, concertedly and without justification, the entry or permanence of a competitor in a market, association or organization of intermediation.
> (i) To agree, without justification, distribution or exclusive sale.

298. There is no precise definition of "agreement" in the LRCA. However, the law makes it clear that it will include in this definition not only contracts but decisions, recommendations or, in general, any kind of concerted practice.

299. In recent decisions, the Commission has been consistent with the wide approach to the concept of agreement established by the LRCA, declaring that an agreement can be inferred from negotiations and exchanges of correspondence, even if there is no actual executed version of the agreement. It is relevant to note that, under Peruvian law, contracts are formed when both parties express their consent. Only certain contracts require a prescribed form.

300. An agreement is not required to be written for INDECOPI to consider an agreement under the LRCA. In that sense, the LRCA has included not only formal agreements but also decisions (guidelines with binding effects), recommendations (statements without binding effects) and concerted practices (agreements demonstrated by circumstantial evidence and presumptions).

301. Therefore, these restrictions will not only be analyzed in cases of formal written agreements but could also take place in cases where the analysis of evidence and proof would contribute to the identification of the concerted practice. Thus, cases of tacit collusion or conscious parallelism would be analyzed by the Commission as conducts that could, but not necessarily, imply the existence of a concerted practice.

302. The Commission has been consistent with the wide approach to the concept of agreement established by the LRCA, declaring that an agreement can be inferred from negotiations and exchanges of correspondence, even if there is no actual executed version of the agreement.

303. As stated above (*see* Part I, Chapter 3), the test of illegality applicable to "horizontal collusive practices" will depend on the nature of the practice. The application of the absolute prohibition or "Per se" rule is restricted to conducts described

---

(j) To agree or coordinate offers, positions or proposal, or refrain from these during bids or public or private tenders or other forms of public contracting or acquisition provided by the corresponding legislation, as well as public auctions or auction sale.
(k) Other equivalent effect practices seeking for benefits due to different reasons than a greater economic efficiency.

11.2. Absolute prohibitions are those horizontal inter-brand practices that are not supplementary or accessory for other legal agreements, which are aimed:

a) To fix prices or other business or services conditions.
b) To limit the production or sales, particularly, by quotes.
c) To distribute customers, suppliers or geographical zones.
d) To establish positions or abstentions during tenders, bids or other forms of public contracting or acquisition provided in the corresponding legislation, as well as public auctions or auction sales.

11.3. The horizontal collusive practices different to the above-mentioned in the item 11.2 are relative prohibitions.

in Article 11.2 of the LRCA, involving mainly price and commercial conditions fixing (e.g., production, sales) between competitors, as well as bid rigging (i.e., "*Naked cartels*"). According to Article 11.2 of the LRCA, only inter-brand collusive practices will fall under the absolute prohibition, given that they are not ancillary to another lawful agreement or practice. All other collusive practices between competitors are assessed under the "Rule of Reason" or relative prohibition.

A. *Price-Fixing*

304. Price-fixing agreements or horizontal collusive practices intended to fix prices in each market are subject to a "Per se" test of illegality, meaning that the sole existence of the practice will suffice to prove the existence of an anticompetitive infringement, regardless of the effects said practice may have had on the market. This has been set forth expressly by Article 11.2 of the LRCA, as price and commercial conditions fixing has been listed in letter a) of said article.

305. As it is expected, hard evidence is rarely found on these types of practices, due to their secrecy and confidential nature. Prima facie evidence is sometimes the only indication of anticompetitive conduct; therefore, INDECOPI tends to rely heavily on economic evidence (price series). While this is somewhat tolerated under the general provisions that regulate the administrative sanctioning procedure in Peru (mainly Law No. 27444), the evidentiary burden relies on INDECOPI and therefore the competition agency must be able to prove that the market behavior found would not be possible in a competitive scenario.

306. Perhaps the seminal and most important case involving price-fixing is the one initiated ex officio by INDECOPI against a group of poultry producers and their trade association (Asociación Peruana de Avicultura) for fixing the price of frozen whole chickens and other commercial conditions in the mid-1990s. By its Resolution No. 276-97-TDC/INDECOPI of November 1997, INDECOPI's Tribunal established the following criteria:

> Pursuant to the rules contained in Legislative Decree 701, prices fixing, market share distribution, production quota distribution and restriction or control of production must be punished according to the "per se" rule. This implies that the mere execution of the forbidden practice constitutes an administrative offense that must be punished as provided by law. In that line, to configure the violation, it is not necessary to consider the damage that the practice may cause to the market or its reasonability, that is, whether it may produce or not the mentioned negative effects.

307. In the last decade, there have been several price-fixing cases resolved by INDECOPI that have been linked to the urban and inter-provincial transportation market, involving recommendations issued within members of transport companies' trade associations, aimed at increasing and/or maintaining transportation tickets at certain levels.

308. In recent years, the most relevant price-fixing cases have been linked to the retail fuel market (serving stations). For instance, in 2018, INDECOPI sanctioned sixty-three companies dedicated to the sale of Vehicular Natural Gas (VNG) and twenty-nine of their officers for fixing the selling prices of VNG in Lima and Callao between July 2011 and May 2015. The Commission determined that the cartel imposed an overcharge of up to 38% per cubic meter (m^3) of VNG sold. The Commission sanctioned the concerned economic agents and their officers with a total fine of 114,594 Tax Units (approx. USD 122 million for 2021).[72] This decision is currently under appeal before the Tribunal.

309. Between 2017 and 2018, INDECOPI also issued its decisions regarding three Liquefied Petroleum Gas (LPG) cartels and one diesel cartel. The LPG cartels concerned price-fixing among gas serving stations in the cities of Chiclayo and Chimbote, and price-fixing among sellers of LPG cylinders for domestic use nationwide. The first two cases were sanctioned with a total fine of 15,545 Tax Units (approx. USD 16 million for 2021)[73] and 2,081 Tax Units (approx. USD 2 million for 2021),[74] respectively. The participants of the LPG cylinder cartel were sanctioned with a total fine of 11,756 Tax Units (approx. USD 12 million for 2021).[75] All these cases were later ratified by INDECOPI's Tribunal.

310. A couple of cases involving price-fixing agreements have been related to the retail market for consumer goods such as pharmaceutical products, which has led INDECOPI to analyze the "*Hub and Spoke*" theory and its intersection with Retail Price Management practices.

311. Moreover, in recent years, INDECOPI's cartel busting efforts have been particularly linked to leniency applications.

B. Market/Client Allocation

312. Market/client allocation horizontal collusive practices are subject to a "Per se" test of illegality, meaning that the sole existence of the practice will suffice to prove the existence of an anticompetitive infringement, regardless of the effects said practice may have had on the market. This has been set forth expressly by Article 11.2 of the LRCA, as market/client allocation has been listed in letter c) of said article.

313. A very important case on the matter was the ex officio administrative procedure initiated by INDECOPI against a group of medicinal oxygen providers in December 2006. PRAXAIR PERÚ S.R.L. (Praxair), AGA S.A. (Aga) and MESSER GASES DEL PERÚ S.A. (Messer) were accused of a geographic market allocation

72. Resolution No. 104-2018/CLC-INDECOPI available in Spanish at: https://bit.ly/3qCtFBt.
73. Resolution No. 101-2017/CLC-INDECOPI available in Spanish at: https://bit.ly/3h3lU4f.
74. Resolution No. 099-2017/CLC-INDECOPI available in Spanish at: https://bit.ly/3qNEHnz.
75. Resolution No. 100-2017/CLC-INDECOPI available in Spanish at: https://bit.ly/3h2i0bL.

agreement in several public tenders for the acquisition of medical oxygen issued by EsSalud (Peruvian Social Security Entity) from 1999 to 2004. This conduct was penalized as an infraction of Article 6 of the Legislative Decree No. 701 (former Competition Law). In August 2010, the Commission ruled on the case,[76] concluding that the defendants were responsible for an agreement that restricted competition.

314. This decision was appealed by the three defendants before the Tribunal, which in July 2013 confirmed the Commission's decision and ordered to pay the following fines:[77]

- Praxair: 3836.82 UIT[78] (this is the largest fine in INDECOPI's history).
- Aga: 1288.14 UIT.[79]
- Messer: 493.84 UIT.[80]

315. According to the Tribunal the medicinal oxygen public bids issued by EsSalud had characteristics that favored the adoption and implementation of a horizontal cartel, such as:

(1) Structural characteristics, related to the existence of high entry barriers restricting the entry of new competitors and a high level of concentration in the market during the period research that facilitated the reduction of transaction costs for implementing a cartel.
(2) Supply characteristics, such as the homogeneity of the medical oxygen required by EsSalud, which facilitated the execution of the agreement by reducing transaction costs.
(3) Features related to the medical oxygen demand, such as the low substitutability of the product, the demand growth and the defendant's market power.

316. The Tribunal confirmed that in the public bids granted by EsSalud between January 1999 and June 2004, several facts were duly proved, and they all constitute a plurality of indicators that, taken as a whole, allow inferring that a restrictive practice took place among the medicinal oxygen providers:

(1) The defendants always offered the best price for the tenders issued for some specific areas, but not for the other regions. Aga catered to the north of Peru, Messer to the center and Praxair to the south and Lima city.

76. Decision No. 051-2010/CLC-INDECOPI, *available at*: https://www.indecopi.gob.pe/documents/20182/143803/Res051-2010.pdf.
77. Decision No. 1167-2013/SDC-INDECOPI, *available at*: http://servicio.indecopi.gob.pe/buscadorResoluciones/getDoc?docID=workspace://SpacesStore/61f24983-fd53-42b2-abd4-90b402f6a5ca.
78. UIT = "Tax Reference Unit." Approx. fine USD 5,100,000.
79. Approx. USD 1,700,000.
80. Approx. USD 660,000.

(2) In the tenders carried out during a first stage (1999-2002), the defendants won offering prices close or equal to 110% of the reference value, the maximum value according to law.
(3) In areas where the defendants did not usually win, they frequently offered prices above the maximum legal allowed (110% of reference value) during the first stage, leading to their disqualification from the bid.
(4) The defendants did not supply oxygen to EsSalud in regions that were geographically closer to their production and filling plants, and where the supply of oxygen would be theoretically more advantageous.
(5) The defendants changed their pattern of behavior since public bidding 0199L00052 granted in September 2002 in which EsSalud eliminated entry barriers in order to favor the entrance of new competitors.

317. Thus, considering the joint analysis of the evidence and given that the alternative explanations offered by the defendants were discarded, the Tribunal concluded that the only possible explanation for the behavior observed in the investigated period was the existence of a restrictive agreement executed by the defendants.

318. Another important case in the past years is the administrative procedure initiated by INDECOPI against six shipping lines that, through a secret agreement, distributed clients (manufacturers or importers of cars and trucks) for the maritime transport of vehicles of various brands.

319. This cartel operated between 2001 and 2012 and affected contracts lasting until 2015. In its final decision, INDECOPI's Antitrust Commission stated that these companies violated Article 11.2 of the LRCA by participating in a system or coordinated understanding which resembled a market allocation practice, since each cartel member would refrain from contacting the other member's clients, with whom they had contracts to transport vehicles on specific routes.[81]

320. In that way, whenever a manufacturer or importer invited shipping companies to present themselves for a tender or requested prices from them, the customer's "owner" shipping line coordinated with its potential competitors, so that they would refrain from participating, offer higher prices than the "owner" or offer less attractive conditions.

321. As a result, six companies: Compañía Marítima Chilena S.A. (CMC), Eukor Car Carrier Inc. (Eukor), Kawasaki Kisen Kaisha Ltd. (K-Line), Mitsui O.S.K. Lines Ltd. (MOL) and Nippon Yusen Kabushiki Kaisha (NYK) were found responsible and sanctioned with fines. Compañía Sudamericana de Vapores S.A. (CSAV) was exonerated from the corresponding fine due to its collaboration under the Leniency Program. The Antitrust Commission imposed fines for a total of 11,529.46 UIT (approx. USD 12 million for 2021):

81. Decision N° 030-2018/CLC-INDECOPI, *available at*: https://bit.ly/3gCHSe3.

– CMC: 19.35 UIT (approx. USD 20,500 for 2021)
– Eukor: 4,189.60 UIT (approx. USD 4 million for 2021)
– K-Line: 2,223.30 UIT (approx. USD 2 million for 2021)
– MOL: 1,916.86 UIT (approx. USD 2 million for 2021)
– NYK: 3,180.36 UIT (approx. USD 34 million for 2021).

322. The most recent case on the matter is the procedure initiated by INDECOPI's Antitrust Commission against a group of companies in the textbook printing services.

323. Metrocolor S.A. (Metrocolor), Corporación Gráfica Navarrete S.A. (Navarrete), Quad/Graphics Perú S.A. (Quad Graphics), Grupo Editorial El Comercio S.A. (El Comercio) and Amauta Impresiones Comerciales S.A.C. (Amauta) were accused of bid rigging several public tenders for the provision of school textbooks from 2009 to 2016.

324. On May 2021,[82] the Commission issued its Resolution No. 015-2010/CLC-INDECOPI declaring that four out of the five defendants were responsible for a horizontal agreement and imposed the following fines:

– El Comercio—Amauta: 4,664.50 Tax Units (approx. USD 5 million for 2021)
– Metrocolor: 2,851.82 Tax Units (approx. USD 3 million for 2021)
– Navarrete: 667.27 Tax Units (approx. USD 740,000 for 2021)
– Quad Graphics: 2,276.82 Tax Units (approx. USD 2 million for 2021).

325. The Commission's decision also fined eight former employees of the companies for their participation in the conduct under investigation, for a total of approximately USD 167,000 for 2021.

326. As it was made public, the case was initiated because of a leniency application by the Grupo El Comercio and Amauta, who are part of the same group, as well as Metrocolor. The decision is currently under appeal by some of the defendants.

C. Production/Innovation Limitation

327. An agreement or concerted practice aimed at restricting production (or sales) or innovation (commercial or service conditions) would be considered "Per Se" illegal by INDECOPI, given that it would fall under the categories set forth in letters a) and b) of Article 11.2 of the LRCA.

328. The case initiated ex officio by INDECOPI against the poultry producers (*see* Price-Fixing) also involved members of the trade association agreeing to limit their poultry production, after discussing the possibility of a significant decrease in

82. Resolution No. 015-2010/CLC-INDECOPI, available in Spanish at: https://bit.ly/3odiZaU.

the level of prices of poultry because of "chicken overproduction" in the national market. Poultry producers also agreed on certain aspects of their offer, including weight or quantities, to increase prices. Evidence indicated that some of the cartel members agreed to restrict fertile egg imports, freeze poultry that exceeded certain quota assigned and discard reproductive hens that exceeded certain quota.[83]

D. Group Boycott

329. Group boycott cases are not included among those practices subject to the absolute prohibition and "Per Se" rule of Article 11.2 of the LRCA but would fall under letter h) of Article 11.1 of the LRCA, as said practices are intended to hinder or restrict the entry or permanence of a given competitor in the market. These practices are assessed under a "Rule of reason" as they are considered relative prohibitions.

E. Collusion on Other Objects

330. Collusive practices other than those expressly established in Article 11.2 of the LRCA would be considered relative prohibitions and therefore fall under a "Rule of reason" approach, demanding that the effects of the practice in the market be pondered in addition to proving the existence of the practice. Unlike the list given in Article 11.2, Article 11.1 includes an extensive list of conducts that include intra-brand collusive practices (e.g., price-fixing, bid rigging) and concerted practices that are ancillary to a lawful agreement.

331. Other practices under this article included concerted refusals to deal, concerted price or commercial conditions discrimination, concerted bundling and so on. As a rule, any practice conducted by a group of competitors that would be considered an abuse of dominance if conducted by a single undertaking will be considered a horizontal collusive practice under the "Rule of Reason" if it does not fall under the list set forth in Article 11.2. Unlike said article, the list provided in Article 11.1 is not closed but includes any other practice that has an equivalent effect on competition and that seeks benefit based on reasons other than economic efficiency.

II. Information Exchange Practices

332. The exchange of sensitive commercial information between competitors would be considered a practice that facilitates horizontal collusion and therefore could be sanctioned as a horizontal collusive practice by itself under Article 11.1. This is because a recent amendment to Article 11.1 in September 2015 (Legislative

83. Page 14 of Resolution No. 276-97-TDC.

Decree No. 1205) replaced the word "agreement" with "collusive practice," extending the application of the "Per Se" rule to any collusive practice that aimed to restrict competition, which includes the exchange of sensitive commercial information.

333. Regarding what kind of information would be considered "sensitive," it is expected that any exchange of information that reduces the natural uncertainty that must prevail between competitors in a competitive environment would be considered anticompetitive for INDECOPI.

334. To this date, however, the exchange of sensitive commercial information has not been sanctioned by INDECOPI as an anticompetitive practice by itself but assessed as prima facie evidence of horizontal collusion.

335. In 2019, INDECOPI's Antitrust Commission published the Guidelines on Trade Associations and Competition,[84] which includes recommendations to associations (guilds, federations, chambers, societies, and professional associations) and their members to identify and prevent practices that can increase the risks of anticompetitive coordination among its members and market exclusion.

336. The Guidelines establish that sensitive information that generally promotes or facilitates the formation of cartels usually relates to the following:

(1) The announcement of immediate or future prices.
(2) The announcement of volumes to be produced, imported or marketed.
(3) Disclosure of cost structures.
(4) Disclosure of customer lists.
(5) Disclosure of business strategies, expansion plans, investment or contracting with the public sector.
(6) Disclosure of trading and contracting terms, including discounts and payment terms

337. For these purposes, INDECOPI recommends that economic agents must not require or exchange the aforementioned information within an association. It also recommends that the agents limit themselves to exchange historical, public, and aggregated information, and that they resort to third-party processing services with the corresponding access limits whenever possible.

III. Cooperation Agreements

338. As stated above, the "Per Se" rule will be applicable to a limited list of horizontal collusive practices that fall under Article 11.2 (i.e., *Naked Cartels*), whereas the "Rule of Reason" will be applicable to those that fall under Article 11.1.

84. Available in English at: https://bit.ly/3xkMETH.

Being that the case, cooperation agreements between competitors could be considered horizontal collusive practices that may fall under one of these two categories, depending on the specific characteristics of the cooperation agreement (e.g., intra- or inter-brand nature).

339. As a general rule, INDECOPI is likely to evaluate a cooperation agreement under a "Rule of Reason" test of illegality, as its effects on competition are not as restrictive as those of "*Naked Cartels*" and therefore should not fall under the same treatment. This benevolent treatment is consistent with that given in other jurisdictions.

340. It must be mentioned that according to the "ancillary" doctrine followed by INDECOPI and recognized by Article 11.2, an agreement that is ancillary to a lawful agreement will not be considered "Per Se" unlawful and therefore would be assessed under the "Rule of Reason." The lawful objective or agreement in each of the cases below would seek market efficiency and consumer welfare, such as the introduction of innovation in the market or research that would otherwise not take place.

A. Research and Development

341. As far as we are aware, there has not been any specific ruling on this matter by INDECOPI since the application of the LRCA. However, as stated above, it is likely that INDECOPI would give a cooperation agreement destined to conduct joint research and product development a benevolent treatment under the "Rule of Reason," given the possible favorable outcome to consumer welfare.

B. Specialization

342. As far as we are aware, there has not been any specific ruling on these matters by INDECOPI since the application of the LRCA. However, as stated above, it is likely that INDECOPI would give a specialization agreement a benevolent treatment under the "Rule of Reason," given the possible favorable outcome to consumer welfare as well as pro-competitive effects.

C. Standardization

343. As far as we are aware, there has not been any specific ruling on these matters by INDECOPI since the application of the LRCA. However, as stated above, it is likely that INDECOPI would give a standardization agreement a benevolent treatment under the "Rule of Reason," given the possible favorable outcome to consumer welfare as well as pro-competitive effects.

D. Joint Production

344. As far as we are aware, there has not been any specific ruling on these matters by INDECOPI since the application of the LRCA. However, as stated above, it is likely that INDECOPI would give a joint production agreement a benevolent treatment under the "Rule of Reason," given the possible favorable outcome to consumer welfare as well as pro-competitive effects.

E. Joint Purchasing

345. As far as we are aware of, there has not been any specific ruling on these matter by INDECOPI since the application of the LRCA. However, as stated above, it is likely that INDECOPI would give a joint purchasing agreement a benevolent treatment under the "Rule of Reason," given the possible favorable outcome to consumer welfare as well as pro-competitive effects.

346. Notwithstanding the foregoing, it must be noted that the Commission has issued a set of criteria in past rulings that would indicate a certain pattern toward the aforementioned benevolent treatment. For example, in Resolution No. 001-97-INDECOPI-CLC of January 1997 (Poultry producers' cartel), the Commission sanctioned a price and commercial conditions fixing cartel, which involved a joint purchasing agreement for chicken feed. The agreement was not sanctioned by itself, but as an agreement facilitating price-fixing and other kinds of anticompetitive collusion practices.

347. Unlike those agreements destined to restrict competition and increase prices, joint purchasing agreements are expected to produce the inverse outcome, as the introduction of efficiency in the market will result in a price decrease that would in turn benefit consumers and promote competition.

348. The Commission issued its Resolution No. 019-2016/CLC-INDECOPI of February 2016, in which it analyzed a bid-rigging cartel involving the provision of hemodialysis services to national hospitals by a group of thirty-four providers. Within the procedure, some of the providers contested that communication and information sharing between them would be justified by the need to conduct joint purchases of medical supplies.

349. Although the existence of a joint purchasing agreement was never under investigation nor proven, the Commission assessed whether the exchange of information was necessary to execute said agreement. The Commission concluded that the exchange of information involving costs of common medical supplies was not ancillary to a hypothetical joint purchase of said products. By conducting this analysis, the Commission is accepting that a joint purchase agreement cannot be considered "Per Se" unlawful. Moreover, the Commission expressly stated that joint purchasing agreements would result in cost reductions that are beneficial to consumers.

F. Joint Selling

350. As far as we are aware, there has not been any specific ruling on these matters by INDECOPI since the application of the LRCA. However, as stated above, it is likely that INDECOPI would give a joint selling agreement a benevolent treatment under the "Rule of Reason," given the possible favorable outcome to consumer welfare as well as pro-competitive effects.

§2. Vertical Agreements

351. The LRCA does not define "vertical restraints" or provide them with a specific characterization for antitrust purposes. Under the LRCA, vertical restraints can be analyzed either as a form of vertical collusion (e.g., agreements, recommendations) or as an abuse of dominant position that involves an agent on a lower or upper level of the commercialization chain.

> Article 12.—Vertical collusive practices.—
>
> 12.1. Vertical collusive practices are those agreements, decisions, recommendations or concerted practices carried out by economic agents operating in different levels of the production, distribution or commercialization chain, aiming to restrict, prevent or distort the free competition.
> 12.2. The illegal vertical conducts may consist on those typified as reference in the items 10.2 of Article 10 and 11.1 of Article 11 of this Law, as applicable.
> 12.3. The configuration of a vertical collusive practice requires at least that one of the involved parties has, previous to the practice, a dominant position in the relevant market.
> 12.4. The vertical collusive practices are relative prohibitions (rule of reason).

352. As further developed in the next chapter, an abuse of dominant position is deemed to have occurred when a firm with dominant position (market power) uses such position to restrict competition, obtaining benefits and harming actual or potential, direct, or indirect competitors. According to the LRCA, to be sanctioned abuses of dominant position shall always be of an exclusionary nature and can consist of conducts such as refusals to deal, discrimination practices, tying, limiting market access or membership to organizations and associations, exclusive distribution or exclusive dealing, non-competition agreements, abuse of judicial and other governmental proceedings (sham litigation) and, in general, of any conduct that may harm or limit competition for reasons other than efficiency.

353. On the other hand, the LRCA defines vertical collusion as agreements, decisions, recommendations or, in general, any kind of concerted practice executed by economic agents operating at different levels of the production, distribution or supply chain, with the purpose of limiting, restricting or harming competition. The LRCA only condemns cases of vertical collusion in which one or more parties have a dominant position (market power).

354. Given that vertical collusion is only prohibited if one or more of the participating parties have a dominant position (market power) in the relevant market, both the analysis of vertical collusions and abuse of dominant position require the assessment of market power. The assessment of market power is further developed in the next chapter.

355. Vertical restraints between affiliates or subsidiaries (and thus between parent and related companies) will not be deemed "agreements" (or concerted practices) under the LRCA. This does not mean that these kinds of vertical restraints are exempted from antitrust scrutiny. In these cases, a group of companies will be treated as a single entity, and thus these practices will be analyzed under the rules regulating unilateral conduct (abuse of dominant position).

356. Antitrust regulations do not provide us with the standard to be applied to determine whether companies should be considered related or not. General regulations on securities and banking will apply for referential purposes. In these regulations, the existence of a relationship between companies is set based on the concept of "control," which is defined as the "preponderant and continuous influence in a company's decision-making structure." Control can be either direct (majority voting power in shareholders' meetings) or indirect (e.g., through agreements, usufructs, trusts).

357. In contrast to cases of horizontal collusion and abuses of dominant position, the LRCA does not list the types of conduct that will constitute vertical collusions in violation of the antitrust rules. The LRCA states that vertical collusion can take any of the forms listed for horizontal agreements or abuses of dominant position. The cases of abuses of dominant position enumerated by the law are already outlined above.

358. In addition, according to the LRCA, horizontal collusion (and thus vertical collusion) can consist of price-fixing and other horizontal restraints to sale conditions, restraints to output, sales, investments, or technical developments, market sharing, market division, territorial division, agreements on quality control when these do not stem from domestic or international technical regulations and negatively impact on the consumer, boycott and concerted refusals to deal, concerted discrimination practices, tying, agreements regarding memberships and access, exclusive distribution or exclusive dealing, coordinated bidding and other conduct of equivalent effects which seek to obtain benefits for reasons other than economic efficiency.

359. As can be seen from the previous paragraphs, the figures of vertical collusion and abuses of dominant position established by the law may easily overlap. Few cases have been decided after the enactment of the Legislative Decree No.

1034 in 2008 and thus the criteria that the Commission and the Tribunal will apply to distinguish between such practices is yet to be seen. The definition of agreement should be crucial for the assessment of vertical restraints since the law seems to imply that it will determine if the challenged conduct is treated as vertical collusion or an abuse of dominant position. However, in a recent decision, the Commission has hinted that the existence of an agreement by itself will not determine the characterization of the practice as vertical collusion or an abuse of dominant position.

360. The LRCA will apply to all vertical restraints that have or may have anti-competitive effects in Peru even if the challenged conduct has been executed extra-territorially. There are no known prior cases in which Peruvian antitrust laws have been applied to conduct that has taken place outside of Peruvian borders. Likewise, the LRCA applies to all individuals, companies, joint ventures and in general, to any private or public entity, private or state-owned which undertakes economic activities. Thus, it will apply to public entities if the challenged conduct qualifies as "economic activity." It will not apply to public entities in the exercise of their governmental powers and functions.

361. It is important to say that sectors such as telecommunications, energy, banking, insurance, and transportation are subject to specific sector regulation which does not necessarily deal directly with antitrust concerns but may impact the assessment of vertical restraints under antitrust rules. In analyzing vertical restraints in these sectors, the competition agencies may have to ponder the impact and effects of the specific laws and regulations of each sector on the challenged behavior.

I. Distribution

A. *Exclusive Distributorship*

362. According to Article 12.2 of the LRCA, vertical agreements can consist of any of the practices listed in Article 10.2 (Abuse of Dominant Position) and/or Article 11.1 (Horizontal Collusive Practices). Being that the case, exclusive distribution agreements would fall under letter e) of Article 10.2 (Establishing, Imposing or Suggesting Unjustified Exclusive Distribution or Dealing Contracts, no compete clauses or any other similar to them).

363. It is relevant to note that allegations of an antitrust infringement in connection with actions to prevent sales by unauthorized buyers or sales by authorized buyers in an unauthorized manner can be raised both in administrative proceedings before INDECOPI (aimed at determining the existence of an infringement to antitrust laws) or as a defense in a contract claim. In both cases, INDECOPI is competent to assess if the agreement is illegal under antitrust laws. Contract claims should be stayed until the rendering of a decision over this matter by the agency.

364. The decision of the authority regarding the possibility to enforce the terms of these agreements to prevent sales by unauthorized buyers or sales by authorized buyers in an unauthorized manner will largely depend on the legality of the provision under antitrust laws since, if the provision or agreement is illegal, it will be unenforceable.

B. Exclusive Dealing

365. According to Article 12.2 of the LRCA, vertical agreements can consist of any of the practices listed in Article 10.2 (Abuse of Dominant Position) and/or Article 11.1 (Horizontal Collusive Practices). Being that the case, exclusive dealing agreements would fall under letter e) of Article 10. 2 (Establishing, Imposing or Suggesting Unjustified Exclusive Distribution or Dealing Contracts, no compete clauses or any other similar to them).

366. On the other hand, exclusive buying or restricting the buyer's ability to obtain the supplier products from alternative sources has received a harsh treatment from INDECOPI. Strong pro-competitive reasons are required to justify such agreements. As mentioned above, in a recent decision concerning the cement market, INDECOPI condemned a cement distributor who obligated other distributors to enter into exclusive buying agreements for cement and other products as a condition to apply discounts in prices and volumes, charging higher prices to distributors that were not affiliated with its network.

367. Also, INDECOPI has issued no previous decision that directly addresses restrictions on the buyer's ability to sell non-competing products that the supplier deems "inappropriate." However, considering the existing decisions on vertical restraints and exclusive dealing, it can be expected that these will receive harsh treatment from INDECOPI, where strong pro-competitive reasons will be required to justify such agreements. For example, in a decision concerning the cement market (Distribuidora Norte Pacasmayo, 2005), INDECOPI sanctioned a cement distributor who demanded other distributors to enter into exclusive buying agreements for cement and other products as a condition to apply discounts in prices and volumes, charging higher prices to distributors that were not affiliated to its network.

368. INDECOPI has explicitly stated (*Backus-Ambev* case, dated June 2005) that these kinds of restraints are subject to the "Rule of Reason." In cases involving exclusive dealing, it has indicated that it will take into consideration the following aspects, which may be applicable to agreements restricting the ability of the buyer to sell non-competing products that the supplier deems inappropriate:

- the degree of foreclosure achieved in the market as a result of the restraint;
- duration of the restraint or contractual relationship;
- pro-competitive justifications; and
- balance between pro-competitive and anticompetitive effects.

369. Given that exclusive dealing cases will be assessed as a vertical collusion practice under a relative prohibition, INDECOPI will not sanction or deem any agreement anticompetitive, unless at least one of the parts involved has a dominant position in the market. This goes in hand with the analysis conducted by INDECOPI involving the degree of market foreclosure, since it is unlikely that without a dominant position in the market, any economic agent will be capable of foreclosing it to a point where competition is not possible or hindered in any significant way.

370. A recent important case involves the telecommunications market and the criteria set by OSIPTEL as the competition agency in the sector.

371. In October 2020, OSIPTEL's Tribunal reversed a first instance decision to sanction broadcast satellite provider DirecTV and Peruvian television network Latina for allegedly agreeing to exclude pay television operators—DirecTV competitors—from the possibility of retransmitting Latina's signal during the 2018 FIFA World Cup.[85]

372. According to the first instance decision, Latina's termination of its retransmission contracts with multiple cable operators originated from the subscription of the sub-licensing contract between DirecTV and Latina regarding the rights to broadcast sixty-four FIFA World Cup matches, benefiting Latina with the possibility to retransmit thirty-two additional matches over which it originally had no rights. Based on indicia, such instance determined that both economic agents had agreed to prevent operators from retransmitting the signal, leaving DirecTV as the sole transmitter of the event.

373. However, in its review, the Tribunal determined that the existing indicia were not enough to prove an offering and an acceptance to collude between both parties. Establishing important criteria for the analysis and proof of vertical agreements, and following the European Commission's Guidelines on Vertical Restraints, the Tribunal considered that the practice either had to be concluded through an offering to collude which responded to with the execution of the solicited terms or had to involve some type of coercion from one of the parties. Neither of those conditions was successfully proved by the Collegiate Body.

374. Having determined that the alleged anticompetitive agreement was not sufficiently proved, the Tribunal revoked the USD 1.1 million fine imposed to DirecTV and the USD 740,000 fine imposed on Latina.

375. Finally, it is important to consider that several markets where an undertaking can achieve dominance are subjected to sector regulation which already forbids exclusive dealing (e.g., telecommunications, infrastructure) and promotes open access through specific mandates.

85. Resolution No. 0019-TSC-2020/OSIPTEL available in Spanish at https://bit.ly/3x6sixx.

C. Selective Distribution

376. According to Article 12.2 of the LRCA, vertical agreements can consist of any of the practices listed in Article 10.2 (Abuse of Dominant Position) and/or Article 11.1 (Horizontal Collusive Practices). Being that the case, selective distribution practices could fall under letter a) (Refusal to Deal) or letter b) (Discrimination) of Article 10. 2, being that the undertaking executing the selective distribution (presumably the one with a dominant position in the market) will be denying other individuals or undertakings in the market (distributors) the possibility of distributing its products and competing in the downstream market with those distributors chosen to distribute the products or services.

377. As with previous practices detailed in this chapter, selective distribution agreements will be assessed under the "Rule of Reason" test of illegality being their relative prohibitions under the LRCA. Being that the case, INDECOPI will not sanction or deem any agreement anticompetitive, unless at least one of the parts involved has a dominant position in the market.

378. To this date, we have no information of any case resolved by INDECOPI involving a selective distribution practice but the framework for the analysis should be equal or at least similar to that applied to other practices detailed above (i.e., exclusive distribution or exclusive dealing).

D. Franchising

379. According to Article 12.2 of the LRCA, vertical agreements can consist of any of the practices listed in Article 10.2 (Abuse of Dominant Position) and/or Article 11.1 (Horizontal Collusive Practices). Being that the case, franchising practices are not specifically contemplated in the LRCA; however, they would fall under the general prohibitions established in letter h) of Article 10.2 (any conduct that impedes or hinders access or permanence of actual or potential competitors to the market for reasons other than greater economic efficiency) or letter k) of Article 11.1 (any other practice that seeks to obtain benefits for reasons other than greater economic efficiency).

380. As with previous practices detailed in this chapter, franchising agreements will be assessed under the "Rule of Reason" test of illegality as relative prohibitions under the LRCA. Being that the case, INDECOPI will not sanction or deem any agreement anticompetitive, unless at least one of the parts involved has a dominant position in the market (presumably the franchisor).

381. To this date, we have no information of any case resolved by INDECOPI involving a franchising agreement, but the framework for the analysis should be equal or at least similar to that applied to other practices detailed above (i.e., exclusive distribution or exclusive dealing).

E. Price and Other Kinds of Restrains

382. For the specific case of vertical price restrictions (or resale price maintenance), it is relevant to note that in a recent decision (*Clorox-Quimpac* case, dated March 2009), which did not directly address the subject, INDECOPI has implied that it will not take vertical agreements involving resale price maintenance lightly, as these can be characterized as agreements which have as their purpose to restrict competition.

383. About vertical territorial restrictions, they will be assessed under a rule of reason analysis. There is no sufficient case law to define the particular circumstances under which these restraints will be deemed legal.

384. Notwithstanding the above, it can be expected that agreements which restrict the territory into which a buyer may resell contract products will be subject to a harsh scrutiny under antitrust laws. In *Clorox-Quimpac* case commented lines above (which did not directly address the subject matter), INDECOPI stated that among the principal effects of these agreements is to limit intra-brand competition, which can hinder market integration. It also asserted that these agreements can facilitate vertical collusion.

385. It is relevant to note that, as part of analysis of the restriction, the Commission or Tribunal may assess if restricting the territory into which a buyer may resell contract products entails discriminatory treatment to competitors. As noted above, discriminatory treatment is characterized both as an abuse of dominant position and as a form of vertical collusion and is condemned when it is unjustified and places one or more competitors in a more advantageous position than others. Usual commercial practices, such as sales, discounts and rewards, which can be justified in the context of an exchange or negotiation, will not be deemed illegal if they are applied on a general basis to parties under similar situations.

386. As with other vertical restrictions, restrictions to resell will be assessed under a rule of reason analysis. There is no sufficient case law to define the particular circumstances under which these specific restraints will be deemed legal. However, it can be inferred from a decision (*Clorox-Quimpac* case, March 2009), which did not directly address the subject matter, that agreements which establish limited distribution chains and among these, those that restrict the customers to whom a buyer may resell contract products, will be subject to strict scrutiny under antitrust laws. INDECOPI has asserted that this type of agreement can prevent access from the relevant product to certain competitors, facilitate vertical collusion and reduce intra-brand competition, thus being necessary to weigh the negative effects on competition with strong pro-competitive justifications.

387. Also, as with vertical territorial restraints, as part of the analysis of the conduct itself, the Commission and Tribunal may analyze whether the restrictions to resell entail discriminatory treatment to competitors. As noted above, discriminatory treatment is characterized as an abuse of dominant position or vertical collusion and is condemned when it is unjustified, and it places one or more competitors in a more advantageous position than others.

388. Finally, restrictions on the uses to which a buyer puts the contract products, sales via internet, selective distribution systems and any other kind of vertical restriction, will be assessed under a rule of reason analysis. Notwithstanding, in establishing a sales politics, a firm needs to take into consideration the provisions against discriminatory treatment that condemn different treatment to equivalent conditions when the difference is unjustified and places one or more competitors in a more advantageous position than others. For example, in a decision concerning the cement market, INDECOPI condemned a cement distributor, who obligated other distributors to enter into exclusive buying agreements for cement and other products as a condition to apply discounts in prices and volumes, charging higher prices to distributors that were not affiliated to its network.

II. Technology Licensing

A. Exclusive Distributorship

389. As of this date, there has not been a single case resolved or even initiated by INDECOPI involving technology licensing and exclusive dealing agreements. As stated above, these practices would have to be analyzed under a "Rule of Reason" (Relative prohibitions) test of illegality requiring that at least one of the participants involved in the practice has a dominant position in the relevant market.

B. Exclusive Dealing

390. As of this date, there has not been a single case resolved or even initiated by INDECOPI involving technology licensing and exclusive dealing agreements. As stated above, these practices would have to be analyzed under a "Rule of Reason" (Relative prohibitions) test of illegality requiring that at least one of the participants involved in the practice has a dominant position in the relevant market.

C. Selective Distribution

391. As of this date, there has not been a single case resolved or even initiated by INDECOPI involving technology licensing and selective distribution agreements. As stated above, these practices would have to be analyzed under a "Rule of Reason" (Relative prohibitions) test of illegality requiring that at least one of the participants involved in the practice has a dominant position in the relevant market.

D. Franchising

392. As of this date, there has not been a single case resolved or even initiated by INDECOPI involving technology licensing and franchising agreements. As stated above, these practices would have to be analyzed under a "Rule of Reason" (Relative prohibitions) test of illegality requiring that at least one of the participants involved in the practice has a dominant position in the relevant market.

Chapter 2. Dominant Undertakings' Prohibited Practices

§1. Exploitative Practices

I. Excessive/Unfair Pricing

393. An exploitative practice implies taking advantage of the market power, which directly impacts the consumers or suppliers, for example, though setting "excessive" prices (for selling or buying) or conditions and terms is considered unfair. Contrary to exclusionary practices, exploitative ones do not affect the structure of the market, are not meant to reinforce the market power of the dominant, and do not set in disadvantage to other competitors, for example, through the negative of contract or deny the access to essentials facilities.

394. In short, exploitative conducts do not have an impact on competition but on the buyers or consumers, who would pay "excessive" prices or, in any case, would pay higher prices than other consumers in the same situation.

395. For a conduct to be considered exploitative, an undertaking would have to discriminate between clients or suppliers, offering different prices and/or conditions for the same product or service. Provided clients or suppliers share the same characteristics, the difference in treatment given to them can be assessed as the practice's degree of exploitation..

396. The LRCA does not sanction exploitative practices. Peruvian legislation only sanctions conduct that has an exclusory effect in the market, and exploitative practices cannot damage the competition process. However, as mentioned above, exploitative practices may be sanctioned by the Peruvian Penal Code as hoarding or price gouging, in the context of a national emergency.

397. The estate obligation to facilitate and promote competition implies punishing the abuse of dominant position and anticompetitive agreements. It means to fight against practices destined to exclude competitors from the market or prevent their entrance. In the case of exploitative damages, they only do not constitute an abuse of dominance but create an incentive for competitors to enter the market and obtain the preferences of the consumers with lower prices and variety.

398. This requirement looks to discard cases that do not have anticompetitive rationality and avoid extreme intervention in the parts' freedom to contract. Its elimination, on the contrary, would create an obligation to contract in all levels, giving capacity to the authority to command to contract in cases of refusals that do not have any effect or anticompetitive rationality.

399. If one accepts sanctions for practices that have not benefited the involved party, one would be limiting the freedom to contract without apparent reason. If INDECOPI were to adopt this criterion, it would obtain plenty of room to threaten freedom to contract and force big companies to "support" small ones, turning the rules of competition into a populist system instead of a promoter of efficiency in benefit of consumers. Thus, it would allow the development of a more social competition that fits a social interest.

400. Besides, it would be an unconstitutional criterion. Article 62 of the Constitution guarantees freedom to contract. Only by a constitutional authorization it is possible to limit this contracting faculty. This authorization, in the present case, is stated in Article 61 of the same constitution. But this authorization to limit freedom to contract only allows restricting the conduct if it has by effect and intent to limit free competition. If who supposedly develops the practice does not have any benefit from this, as stated by the law, it is not understood how this could be a reason for a generic authorization to limit the right to contract.

401. However, in a case that took place almost two decades ago, INDECOPI's Tribunal did precisely the contrary to what the economic logic, and particularly the norm, establishes. The case in which this occurred was that contained in Resolution No. 0869-2002/TDC-INDECOPI, dated December 11, 2002, that collects the decision in the claim posed by CAB CABLE against ELECTROCENTRO.

402. The case refers to the complaint presented by CAB CABLE, a company that provides cable television services in the city of Huancayo, against ELECTROCENTRO, a power distribution company that operates in the same city.

403. To provide cable television services, the complainant had celebrated a contract with ELECTROCENTRO to use the poles that the company used for its net. Once the contract expired, ELECTROCENTRO refused to sign a new contract, claiming that commercial circumstances had changed and that it was impeded to do so by quality regulations applicable to its power distribution service. The defendant company pointed out that its poles did not have adequate characteristics to provide the service, which had generated a series of technical inconveniences during the execution of the contract.

404. It is worth mentioning that ELECTROCENTRO, in its claim of defense, left clear that its negativity to contract even damaged itself, because it deprived it of receiving the additional revenue that the rent of the poles would imply. Thus, it claimed that its refusal to contract was founded on an operative-commercial decision.

405. As follows from the case's facts, the question that arises is whether INDECOPI can get itself involved in a relationship of a private nature, sustained in commercial decisions between companies. The answer can only be affirmative if behind the practice lies an anticompetitive motivation.

406. It was clear, however, that ELECTROCENTRO did not have any interest in the market of cable television. Neither ELECTROCENTRO nor any linked company provides such service. The only thing that occurs because of the refusal is the loss of an additional income. Therefore, the reasonability and justification of such refusal are presumed, which are obtained by proving that ELECTROCENTRO receives some benefit.

407. However, in this case, the Tribunal stated that "(…) the exercise of the private autonomy enjoyed by the parties—within the frame of public economic order protected by the right to compete—cannot harm the equality between competitors nor the legitimate interests of consumers."

408. This decision was widely criticized since it implied an expropriation and a violation of private autonomy of ELECTROCENTRO, without any anticompetitive behavior on its part.

409. Considering the aforementioned, the LRCA expressly excludes exploitative practices as a punishable conduct by establishing in its Article 10.2 that an abuse of dominant position in the market consists of conducts of exclusionary effects.

410. The impossibility of sanctioning "exploitative" practices in Peru has also been established jurisprudentially.

411. On March 16, 2011, in a case involving the milk market, the Competition Tribunal confirmed a decision of the Commission which dismissed Agalep and Fongal complaints against Gloria, the most important dairy products company in Peru. The plaintiffs considered that Gloria had abused its dominant position in the market for the acquisition of fresh milk to producers. As they argued, Gloria was paying them "abusively low prices" and had generated a discriminatory incentives scheme, as well as manipulated the milk quality analysis system.

412. With its decision, the Tribunal closed a long-term debate about the viability of sanctioning conducts not only with exclusionary effects but also with exploitative ones. According to the Tribunal's decision, the alleged conducts could not produce any real or potential exclusion of Gloria's competitors, but only had an exploitative effect. In that vein, considering that the conducts were not able to affect the competitive process, this could not be considered as an abuse of dominant position case.[86]

---

86. According to the LRCA, there could be an abuse of dominant position if the conduct has exclusionary effects:

> Article 10.—Abuse of Dominant Position.—
> 10.1. It is considered that there is abuse when an economic agent being in a dominant position within the relevant market uses such position to restrict inappropriately the competition, obtaining benefits in detriment of real or potential, direct or indirect, competitors, which would not have been possible without being in such dominant position.
> 10.2. The abuse of dominant position in the market may consist on conducts of exclusionary effects such as (…).

II. Discrimination

413. As any other conduct involving abuse of dominance, discrimination is a practice subject to the "Rule of Reason." This means, it will only be deemed as illegal if it can be demonstrated that it hinders or negatively affects competition in the market and in consumer welfare.

414. Price discrimination[87] can be defined, in general terms, as a situation in which units of a same good or service are commercialized at different prices,[88] which means: the same good is sold at different prices. That difference can be determined by comparing the price of the good or service regarding different consumers or in operations made by the same supplier.[89]

415. It is considered that price discrimination can have a negative effect on competition when it is used as a mechanism to exclude other competitors from the market or to prevent new competitors from entering the market. For example, through granting "special prices" to clients who are targeted by a new competitor with the deliberate purpose of inhibiting its access to the market and facilitating the subsequent price increase. That could occur, for example, in some cases, if a dominant undertaking were to raise its prices only to clients who also buy from its competitor.

416. Because of this, in Peru, discrimination is not sanctioned as an exploitative practice but only as an exclusionary practice and is therefore subjected to the "Rule of Reason" as any other abuse of dominance practice or vertical restraint. In this sense, Article 10.2 of the LRCA establishes:

> The following constitute cases of abuse of dominant position: (...)
>
> b) Applying, in commercial relations or service relations, unequal conditions to equivalent provisions that place without justification, some competitors in a disadvantageous way towards others. It does not constitute abuse of dominant position, providing discounts or extra payments that correspond

---

87. The price discrimination is one of many practices of establishment of non-uniformed prices, as well as the tariff in two parts, the establishment of discounts per quantities, tied sakes and the discrimination per quality.
88. Units that are physically equal can be considered as different goods according to their different costs of production, when commercialized in different markets. This way, the sale of equal goods at different prices is not a case of price discrimination unless those goods are produces at identical costs.
89. There are three types of price discrimination. In first place, the first-degree or perfect discrimination takes place when the company can charge a different price to each consumer according to what he is willing to pay for the good. It has by purpose the extraction of all the surplus of the consumer. On the other hand, the second-degree discrimination is characterized by the non-intention of adjusting the prices to the elasticity of the consumers' demands, as the prices structure is the same for all of them. Last, the third-degree decimation differs from the case before as the company cannot identify the will of pay of each consumer, and due to that, it discriminates prices between consumers of totally independent groups or markets. The company can identify the elasticity of the demands on the different groups or markets and adjust the price according to that, charging a lower price to consumers whose demand is most sensible.

> to commercial practices generally accepted, that are conceded or provided under some particular compensatory circumstances, such as the anticipated payment, amount, volume or others that are provided in general, in every case in which equal conditions exist (…)

417. As shown, the general principle established by the LRCA is that discrimination will be deemed illegal only under the following concurrent conditions:

(1) That the company that performs the discrimination has a dominant position.
(2) That the practice generates anticompetitive effects in the market.

418. The LRCA further defines discrimination as the application of "unequal conditions to equal provisions." Meaning that the application of different market conditions can be justified in the difference between clients or suppliers, provided that those differences are based on objective commercial, economic, or technical grounds.

419. On this basis, it can be deduced that the law does not penalize providing differentiated treatment based on the existence of conditions that justify such differentiation, as volumes of sale, anticipated payment, or other similar conditions. Indeed, a differentiated treatment can justify itself in economic reasons or other elements objectively identifiable, which can relate to conditions of the operation, supply or the demand.[90]

---

90. The existence of differences in the level of the demand has been considered in previous INDECOPI resolutions as sufficient justification for the establishment of a differentiated commercial treatment. For example, Resolution No. 001-98-INDECOPI-CLC from the Jan. 9, 1998, the proceeding followed between the National Industry Society against the Company "Minera del Centro del Perú S.A.," established the following:

> 3.5. The Commission considers that from a legal point of view, the geographical price differentiation does not result to be punishable by it, as the price differentiation existent could be justified by the existence of differentiated costs – transaction or transportation costs for example-, or for being about operations made in different markets, in which the consumers count with a different elasticity in the demand, that would reflect a different degree of substitution of the good or the access to supplying sources.

Similarly, in Resolution No. 007-1999/TDC-INDECOPI emitted by the Courtroom in the proceeding followed by the Newspaper *El Comercio* against Aero Continente for abuse of dominant position in the way of price discrimination, the following was said:

> When a situation of restriction in the offer of the service takes place, the conditions of the market described before determine that those companies that require to hire air freight and cargo service of immediate nature, must be able to pay a high price for this kind of service. This higher price reflects the cost of excluding every other types of cargo that compete to access the air transportation service. This occurs in the case of the service of diaries and magazine distributions. The companies that distribute this type of products are willing to pay more for the transport in the morning flights that the price that those companies that send other type of cargo are willing to pay (including the case of perishing goods such as shellfishes). This explains why the raise of prices affects more the cargo transport of diaries and magazines.

420. Bearing in mind that we are in front of a behavior that only under certain circumstances can generate anticompetitive effects, the LRCA has restrained the discrimination to the denominated *rule of reason*, which requires INDECOPI to evaluate the illegal character of the practice over the basis of the same reasonableness in the concrete case. If there are no elements of judgment that make us presume that the costs of the practice exceed the benefits of it, the practice must be considered legal and in consequence, be free of sanction.

421. Discrimination can be defined in general terms as a situation in which units of the same goods or services are sold at different prices or dissimilar conditions.

422. Exploitative discrimination is an example of an arbitrary practice, which, as has been mentioned above, consists of the direct exercise of market power. Through this conduct, the dominant undertaking imposes on its customers or suppliers different conditions to obtain greater economic benefits.

423. Exploitative behaviors, such as discrimination, do not affect the competitive process. On the contrary, they make it more dynamic, encouraging the entry of new competitors who may be attracted by dominant earnings, as well as permit the products or services to be enjoyed by a wider spectrum of clients (this explains, for example, why a cinema charges a lower price to kids and old persons).

424. The Commission has established in several opportunities[91]that price differentiation will not be sanctioned if there are not exclusionary effects. INDECOPI's Tribunal has also stated the aforesaid in *Fongalsur v. Gloria S.A.*,[92] in which it was established that it is possible to apply dissimilar conditions to services which are apparently similar. Different conditions become illegal only where they are aimed to, or have the effect of, restrict competition.

In consequence, the Tribunal considers that the differentiation of tariffs questioned by El Comercio is explained because Aero Continente has identified a special nature services demand, constituted by the air freight and cargo of diaries and magazines. That demand requires handling merchandises daily and immediately, in the first morning flights. This way, given the particular conditions of the service required, the accused has established a special tariff for the transportation of diaries and magazines that the Courtroom considers justified.

This way, according to the criteria exposed in point III.2 of the present resolution, if reasonable explanations for the differentiated prices policy established by a company exist and if, on the other hand, from the analysis of the facts, the aim of restricting competition is not appreciated, the practice should be considered licit. It must be taken in count that, if not, the application of the regulations contained in Legislative Decree No. 701 would conduct to a system veiled of price control that finally, would produce a bigger distortion in the resources assignment in the market.

91. (i) *Fund for the Development of South Dairy Farming (Fongal Sur, acronym in Spanish) v. Gloria S.A.* (1993); (ii) *El Comercio S.A., v. Aero Continente S.A.* (1999); (iii) *Association of Gas BaggersPeru (ASEEG, acronym in Spanish) v. VopakSerlipsa S.A. y Petróleos del Perú S.A.* (Petroperú) (2007).
92. Resolution No. 003-93-INDECOPI/CLC of the Multisectoral Commission of Free Competition of INDECOPI, Aug. 31, 1993, about complaint made by the "Fund for the Development of South Dairy Farming" (Fongal Sur, acronym in Spanish) against Gloria S.A.

425. In *INEMEC v. SEDAPAL*[93], even though it was determined that SEDAPAL had a dominant position, the authority did not consider the practice as discriminatory since defendants' acquisitions were subject to a set of technical rules. INEMEC, a gates national manufacturer, argued that the inclusion of certain technical requirements in the bidding terms prevented Peruvian manufacturer to participate, which implied discrimination in favor of foreign manufacturers. The Commission considered that it was a lawful requirement that fits "(…) with the quality and safety that the Estate must fulfill because of the work to be executed (…)." As well, it was established that "(…) the existence of a discrimination act is not detected, and we cannot conclude that the bidding terms were written with a discriminatory purpose (…)." Moreover, the Commission recognized the absence of anticompetitive effects.

426. In *Depósitos Santa Beatriz S.R.L. and others v. Distribuidora Norte Pacasmayo S.R.L.*, the latter was accused of setting different conditions for the distributors that held affiliation agreements in comparison with those that did not, for the acquisition of cement and other building materials. The Commission clearly established that the difference in retail prices offered to affiliates and co-affiliates was justified since they also grant benefits to the defendant, such as advertising, exclusive and planned purchases, information flow and cost savings of installing branches. In this vein, it was accredited that the difference in prices had an objective criterion, which is completely justified according to the LRCA. This was also confirmed by the Supreme Court.

427. In *EmpresaEditora El Comercio S.A. v. Aero Continente S.A.*, the authority investigated Aero Continente's decision of charging higher prices to El Comercio (a national newspaper) in comparison with its competitors for the service of newspaper air transportation to provinces. The authority determined that some publishing companies—competitors of El Comercio—had celebrated agreements with Aero Continente in which Aero Continente agreed to grant lower prices for its services in exchange for advertising spaces in their newspapers.

428. In this case, INDECOPI's Tribunal established the following criteria:

> However, the differentiation of prices made by Aero Continente between the different media companies finds its justification in the fact that, before the implementation of its new pricing policy for the transport of newspapers and magazines, the company had celebrated "account exchange" contracts, so that it was not possible to apply in a uniform way the price increases for such services.
>
> Thus, it must be concluded the claim referred to the prices differentiation among companies is also unfounded, given that this practice is justified by the contractual relations that the defendant had previously established with other clients.

93. Resolution No. 30-94-INDECOPI/CLC.

429. Likewise, the claimant company was also invited to participate in the agreements that would have allowed it to access more convenient rates.

§2. Exclusionary Practices

I. Predation

A. *Conditions for Predatory Practices*

430. When price predation occurs, the predator first sells its products or services at a loss to exclude its competitors from the market and then raises its prices above competitive levels to recoup in excess the initial loss.

431. There are three conditions that can make predatory pricing viable: (i) undertaking should have a dominant position, (ii) entry costs to the market should be high; and (iii) predator must be able to recoup losses in a short term.

432. In relation to the first condition, predation will only be sanctioned if it is performed by an agent with dominant position in a particular market. Reasons for that requirement are obvious. An undertaking without dominant position would not be able to bear losses for a certain period and then recover by recouping those losses and gaining the market power left by the excluded competitor. Only agents with sufficient market power can assume those costs. This is one of the differences between predatory pricing and aggressive competition on prices.

433. Analyzing predatory pricing then implies finding that predator incurred in losses during the practice but is in the capacity of making a rational calculation to consider those losses as an investment in the search of monopolistic revenues. Then, expected monopolistic revenues must overcome actual losses.

434. Therefore, one of the basic economic elements that must be necessarily defined is not only that the predator can bear the losses and defeat its competitors but also that it can generate quick and effective profits that can overcome the losses suffered during the predatory period.

435. In open markets and with low entry costs, it is highly unlikely (not to say impossible) that predatory pricing can succeed. Predatory costs might overcome future monopolistic profits. Undertakings could bear losses for months or years trying to exclude a competitor. And even if they succeed, nothing could guarantee that in a short period of time new competitors would not enter the market and control undertaking's monopolistic prices. This looks clearer if we take into consideration that raising prices after price wars create incentives for the entry of new competitors.

436. Under these circumstances, demonstrating that the agent under investigation has a dominant position is very important. However, it is also important to say that undertaking's dominant position could not only exist in the market in which the practice is implemented but also in a different market. For example, if a company with dominant position in Lima's market uses its monopolistic profits in that market to subsidize its entry into Arequipa's market or uses its dominant position in the beer market to subsidize the price of soda's, the market in which it does not have a dominant position. Hence, although predatory pricing could be implemented in the market in which the undertaking has dominant position (to discipline or eliminate competitors), it could also happen in a different market.

437. Regarding the second element and since predatory pricing implies that predator will maintain the power market earned with the removal of the defeated competitor from the market, reentry costs to that market should be high enough to prevent the entry of new competitors. Therefore, predatory pricing is much likely to succeed in markets with high barriers to entry, especially legal barriers as permissions that require investment and stranded costs.

438. Finally, because of initial losses and exclusion of a competitor, a predator must have the possibility to recoup those losses in a short term. Market conditions must allow that possibility. Hence, allegations of long-term predatory pricing should be considered suspicious by the authority.

B. Legal Treatment

439. Peruvian antitrust law does not have an express regulation for predation as a case of abuse of dominant position. However, in a particular case decided in 1996 under the enforcement of the Legislative Decree No. 701 (previous law in force at that time), the Commission stated that even when it had not been expressly regulated, predation practices could be sanctioned when sufficient evidence was found.

440. Under the LRCA, predation practices can be considered in subparagraph b) of Article 10.2 which establishes that applying uneven conditions to similar services or products and clients could be sanctioned as a case of abuse of dominant position. In that case, if a company offers to its clients in Arequipa[94] a lower price than the one offered to its clients in Lima[95] and price discrimination could not be justified for economic reasons, then the conduct could be sanctioned under Article 10.2.b). For that, price discrimination should be aimed to exclude or eliminate actual or potential competitors in Arequipa. Price discrimination then may be understood as a cross-subsidy.

441. Since Article 10.2.b) regulates discrimination it would not be directly applicable if the cross-subsidy is not held between two different geographical markets (Lima and Arequipa) but between two products or services in which monopolistic revenues in one market subsidize prices in the other.

94. Arequipa is one of the principal cities in Peru and it is situated in the south.
95. Capital of Peru.

442. In any case, predatory practices can also be included in the open clause regulated in subparagraph h) of Article 10.2 of the LRCA, which states that the abuse of dominant position could be executed, in general, through conducts that restrain or difficult the access or maintenance of competitors in the market for reasons that are not related with economic efficiency.

443. Predation must be analyzed under the rule of reason or the "relative prohibition," as stated in Article 9 of the LRCA. Therefore, predation will only be sanctioned when competitive effects overrun anticompetitive effects of the practice. This rule should permit the competition authority to identify and distinguish harmful practices from aggressive price competition.

C. Predation Case Law

444. Given the difficulties related to the implementation of predatory pricing, there is not much case law on the matter. However, in a case solved in early 1996, under the Legislative Decree No. 701, the Antitrust Commission of INDECOPI analyzed the possibility of sanctioning predation. In that case, Maria del Carmen Molta Wendell and others argued that a chemical product manufacturer, Productos Químicos S.A.—Proquinsa, had sold sodium silicate with prices below its cost, incurring in losses to damage its competitors.[96]

445. Even though INDECOPI considered that predatory pricing had not been implemented by Proquinsa, the authority went through the analysis of the practice and the requirements for its sanction.

446. The Commission defined predatory pricing as "those [prices] that are lower than certain level of costs, established with the intention to exclude of the market one or several competitors." As can be appreciated, the Commission introduced an intention requirement for the evaluation of the practice.

447. In addition, the effects that the Commission considered derived from predatory pricing are: (i) selective price discounts, (ii) non- or low-profitable prices, and (iii) price policies directed to one specific competitor. These requirements, especially the first and third one show the relation between predatory pricing and price discrimination. Then, as stated before, it could be possible in some circumstances to apply subparagraph b) of Article 10.2 of the LRCA to predatory practices.

448. But the Commission also identified risks related to confusing aggressive price competition with predatory pricing. In that sense, it stated that "it should be taken into account that price competition is a normal an expected characteristic of the competition process. Therefore, price reductions can be a proof of that effective competition even in a market where an agent has dominant position and should not be forbidden only because they damage a certain competitor."

96. Decision No. 070-96-INDECOPI-CLC. Case No. 047-95-CLC.

449. It is important to mention that according to the Commission, not all pricing below cost would be considered predatory pricing. The Commission established that prices should be considered as predatory when they are lower than average variable cost, since variable costs are defined by the production level. Also, prices below total costs but higher than average variable costs would only be considered as predatory if they are part of an exclusionary strategy against one or more competitors. Therefore, the Commission identified that there could be situations in which the intention requirement would not be asked and yet it would be considered as predatory.

450. In the case of Proquinsa, the Commission concluded that prices had been kept above total costs and therefore above variable costs. Given the fact that only one of the months analyzed showed that prices were lower than total costs, the Commission considered that it was not possible to derive a predatory intention from that particular fact. Without the intention requirement it was not possible to sanction Proquinsa. The conduct could be explained with economic or commercial reasons different from an exclusionary intention to harm competition.

451. As it can be appreciated, predatory pricing is not only unusual in the market but also in cases where it is implemented; it will be difficult to find that the conduct has really infringed antitrust law. However, if evidence is sufficient and clear enough to do so, considering the criteria exposed by the Commission and the legal requirements, predatory pricing could be sanctioned.

II. Tying

A. Tying/Bundling and Its Effects on Competition

452. Throughout a tied sale, a seller of various products who has a dominant position in the market in the supply of any of them establishes that the clients will only be able to buy that product (the one that enjoys the dominant position) if they accept to buy a product of a different type (over this second product, the supplier does not have a dominant position). In other words, the seller links or bundles the sale of his products without considering the interest of the buyers toward them. In this understanding, tied sales are defined as: "situations in which the sale of a good is only possible by the purchase of another one."[97]

453. An essential element in the definition of this conduct is the pressure applied over the buyer so that he acquires all the products supplied by the seller, even though the buyer is only interested in buying one specific product of that seller.

454. The sanction imposed to this type of behavior has its origin in the possibility that companies must appeal to this type of activity with the only intention of

97. *Glossary of Terms Relative to the Industrial Organization's Economy and the Antitrust Laws*, World Bank, 1996, p. 57.

extending their market power over a particular market (of the dominant product) to another one (of the tied product). This behavior would allow an agent with dominant position to establish a higher price in the market where it faces a greater competition and eventually excludes from that market the existing competitors. Consequently, tied sales can also be considered as a type of price discrimination: if a company has a dominant position in a particular market and ties the sales of its product to another one in which it does not enjoy the same position, the consumers will be forced to buy the second product if they intend to buy the first one, even though they could purchase it for a lower price from another supplier. In this way, the price charged to each consumer is different.

455. Not all bundling generates negative effects. Usually, tying is a normal and legitimate practice that generates benefits to the market and consumers. In fact, almost every product or service we acquire in the market is nothing but the tying of a group of goods. Take as an example a car: the ties, the engine, the bodywork, etc., are a combination of ensembles provided by the seller that cannot be separated. Other goods, like some accessories, are not strictly tied, but normally the consumer cannot choose to untie them and is forced to receive the product as it has been bundled. Usually, we can spot bundles when by commercial uses, we can distinguish between different goods.

456. This way, there are several circumstances in which tied sales may have positive effects on competition, generating the following positive consequences:

1. Efficiency Increase

457. Tied sales can generate efficiency, as they reduce transaction costs for consumers. For example, as most people do not have preferences about shoelaces, shoes are commonly sold with shoelaces, which are necessary for their use. As consumers must buy both products together, costs are reduced, as it becomes unnecessary to go to another store specifically to buy shoelaces. This means transaction costs are reduced.

458. As we were saying, each product can be understood as the composition of various individual goods. In this way, it is simple to understand that most people consider buying an assembled car more efficient than buying its parts separately, notwithstanding that different levels of competition exist in the markets where each product is sold separately.

2. Assure Quality

459. Tied sales assure quality and the optimum functioning of the sold product. Sometimes, the supplies employed by some machineries or devices are essential to their adequate functioning. Hence, to warrantee the quality of the functions of a smartphone, it will be necessary to count on a series of applications that accomplish certain quality standards. This way, smartphone producers will be compelled to tie a certain number of basic applications to the sale of the smartphone.

460. This is related to the reduction of externalities. In some cases, the use of third-party services or products can damage a supplier or manufacturer, either directly (coverage of contractual warrantees) or indirectly (loss of prestige). If a vehicle breaks down and is still under warranty, the supplier/manufacturer will be responsible for its repair or replacement. The supplier/manufacturer should not bear the cost of repair nor replace the vehicle, if the latter was taken and repaired by a non-authorized workshop, or third-party parts were used in the repair. Because of this, warranties are usually void if consumers failed to use authorized repair centers or authorized parts.

B. Legal Treatment

461. Tied sales are regulated on Legislative Decree No. 1034, as a practice of abuse of dominant position. Clause 10.2 establishes that:

> 10.2. the abuse of the dominant position in the market may consist in excluding effect behaviors such as:
>
> (…)
>
> c) Subordinating the celebration of contracts to the acceptance of additional provisions that, by their nature or commercial use, are not related to the aim of such contracts.

462. A key element in the typifying of the infraction is the "subordination" of one desired provision to the acceptance of another one not desired. We can see here a demanding, pressing or coercion element, which is performed by an agent that has a dominant position over other agents that suffer this practice: an agent is forced to purchase something he does not want. If the agent voluntarily accepts the "subordination" to the provisions—because it reduces the future costs of transaction, or costs of transportation, for example—the infraction does not take place.

463. Another basic component of the typifying of the infraction is referred to the link between the provisions: the law does not forbid any type of conditioning in the sale of a good or service to the acceptance of others. The law refers exclusively to those cases in which the goods or services "tied" are not related among them. This way, for example, the behavior by which a supplier of cars forces his clients to acquire jointly with the car, a replacement tie for it, is not included in this prohibition.

464. As well as the other similar practices displayed in the law, a punishment a priori does not exist for this kind of practices: the sanction must be preceded by an analysis of the negative and positive effects derivative from the behavior, proceeding to sanction the behavior only in cases in which the restrictive effects to the competition overcome the positive aspects.

465. As we mentioned before there are some cases in which it is evident that the tie is efficient, for example, when its aim is to protect the quality or prestige of a product.

466. On other occasions, they are used to accomplish effective price discrimination. Consequently, this practice can be considered abusive just when it is used with the intention of price discrimination. However, we must highlight that price discrimination, in cases of dominant position, can be a positive restrictive practice if it contributes to increase the produced quantity. When discriminating prices, the monopolist production increases, because it can get to clients who would not be able to pay the monopoly price. The effects of this practice over the efficiency are ambiguous.

467. We should also consider that it is difficult to determine when a tying clause exists. For example, sometimes there are offers that state "buy toothpaste and receive for free a toothbrush." As in the market nothing is for free, we could be before a tying clause by which the consumer is compelled to buy both products for only one price that reflects the cost of both. But there is no doubt that it appears as a legitimate commercial practice.

468. In other cases, tying clauses are linked to franchise contracts where the supplier demands the buying of all the integrating elements of it. For example, the franchiser of a hamburger fast food would force the franchisee to buy meat, bread, wrapping, desserts, napkins, beverages, etc. Here, it also seems as if justified reasons exist: to maintain the standardization of the franchised stores. It could be said that the box in which a product is sold determines a bundle with the product itself. It is not a behavior that should ordinarily be sanctioned, and it seems like the cases in which this must take place are exceptional. It would be a case to apply the rule of reason.

C. Tying Case Law

469. Peruvian case law has considered that it is unusual to sanction this type of infraction. We must have in mind that the attempt to monopolize the market implies increasing the cost of the original market, what strangely is a rational behavior. If a consumer values the product "X" in USD 10 (product of the company that enjoys a dominant position) and the price at which it is sold is USD 8, at first, the client would want to buy it. Now, if the monopolist obligates the consumer to buy product "Y" at USD 5, in which he has not got any interest (for him, it is worth USD 0 or very little), the monopolist would be forcing the consumer to pay USD 13 for a package of products that the consumer values in USD 10 as a whole. Evidently, he would not buy the product, with what the monopolist will have lower sales at higher costs.

470. Even if he got to sell the product, he would be reducing his utility margin due to the rise in the cost of providing product "Y." It is more logical to sell only the desired product by the consumer and to charge for it the monopolistic price.

471. One example of this problem can be appreciated in a particular case of the Peruvian market. The Peruvian Official Newspaper called "El Peruano" has the legal monopoly for the publication of the legal norms and regulations. That monopoly forces consumers of the information contained in those regulations (basically lawyers and accountants) to buy the section of El Peruano where the regulations are published called "Boletín Oficial," to have access to that information during the day. But El Peruano has established a bundling clause with the purchase of the journalistic section of the newspaper. It is obvious that the consumer of the legal regulations has got no interest in purchasing the journalistic part; however, as it comes tied to the Boletín Oficial, he has got no choice but to buy it.

472. This clearly shows how such a bundle should make no sense to the newspaper. If the consumer sees no value in the journalistic section but still pays USD 2.00 for the bundle, it is an indication that the value the consumer sees in the Boletín Oficial by itself is over USD 2.00. The newspaper is spending more money in publishing the journalistic part that is not valued and therefore, if it stopped doing so it would lower its costs and increase its profit margin.

473. Normally when one ties one product to another, it is to expect that that bundle will be efficient because it is what consumers expect to receive as a package of products.

474. Another case of this conduct was resolved by the Controversy Court of OSIPTEL. Osiptel accused Telefónica del Perú S.A.A. ("Telefónica") for tying up the sale of its product called "Speedy" (internet access through Asymmetric Digital Subscriber List (ADSL) technology)—market in which Telefónica had a dominant position—to the purchase of the service of landline. This way, Telefónica only accepted to sell Speedy together with its landline, arguing that the ADSL technology was distributed to the users by the copper wires of the landline. Hence, ADSL and landlines would need the same infrastructure. OSIPTEL confirmed the lawsuit, as it proved that there was no way of acquiring the internet service without purchasing the landline, but the landline could be acquired without the internet service. Furthermore, OSIPTEL stated that to sanction this behavior it was necessary to demonstrate that there was an exclusionary effect in the market, affecting the competition process, and going over the positive effects caused by the behavior. Consequently, it was proved that Telefónica caused an exclusionary effect in the market with its conduct, as its landline competitors lost market participation, and barriers to entry increased with the practice.

III. Rebates

475. There is no specific prohibition for rebates of any kind under the LRCA. These practices however could be assessed by INDECOPI under the practice of price discrimination or given their effects, as exclusive distributorship, or exclusive dealing, as previously covered.

476. Because of this, to determine whether a rebate of any kind should be deemed unlawful, INDECOPI will have to assess it under the "Rule of Reason" approach.

477. This will mean that to be unlawful, a rebate of any kind would have to distort or restrict competition (have an exclusionary effect on competitors) to an extent where it surpasses any gains or benefits to the competition structure or consumer welfare. If this cannot be proven, the practice will have to be considered lawful. These practices cannot be considered illegal per se by INDECOPI.

478. In the past, INDECOPI has considered that any competition assessment of "fidelity discounts" should fall under the rule of reason and not the Per Se Rule. In *DINO v. Santa Beatriz*, the then Technical Secretariat issued its Technical Report No. 006-2003-INDECOPI/CLC in which it recognizes that certain benefits to competition and consumer welfare may be obtained through rebates, which requires the practice to be assessed under a "Rule of Reason" approach and not under the Per Se Rule. The Technical Secretariat based its approach on the conclusions set forth at the "Roundtable on Loyalty and Fidelity Discounts and Rebates" organized in Paris in June 2002 by the Organisation for Economic Co-operation and Development (OECD).

479. To assess the "foreclosure" element of the practice, INDECOPI will ponder whether the practice reasonably allows competitors to find alternative supply sources or if the imposition of rebates distorts competition excluding possible competitors from entering or participating in the market.

480. This, for example, was the criteria used by INDECOPI when assessing a claim filed by AMBEV (brewery) against BACKUS (brewery). In this case, INDECOPI considered that BACKUS' conduct destined to grant fidelity rebates to distributors was not anticompetitive, as 30% of the market was not subject to any restrictions imposed by those fidelity rebates and therefore, was open for any competitor to participate.

481. INDECOPI will also have to assess whether there are any economic or commercial justifications to the conduct, regarding efficiency, objectives or effects. The conduct could be justified, for example, by the need to improve services by distributors in the downstream market (consumers) or the existence of common practices in other competitive markets. The burden of proof for justifications and its effects will be higher when the dominant undertaking has a higher market share or higher market foreclosure.

IV. Refusal to Deal

A. An Approach to the Conduct

482. Just as with other practices, refusal to deal is, in principle, a legal conduct. It is an inherent part of every person's free will and freedom to contract. However, when a company has a dominant position, it is subject to certain specific obligations, as is the case of not refusing, without objective reason, to deal with a provider (in case of monopsony) or with a client (in case of a monopoly).

483. Usually, authors had considered concerted refusal to contract, also known as "boycott," like a per se illegal practice. If a group of companies agrees not to hire a company or a competitor, or a specific group of companies or consumers, that will be considered an illegal practice itself, without prejudice of the analysis of its real or potential effects.

484. But unilateral refusal, for example, the one the Company does because of its own decision, brings up a lot of difficulties, because there are several cases in which the practice is perfectly comprehensible and reflects market conditions.

485. The refusal does not necessarily have to be explicit and clear. More sophisticated refusal forms are just not to respond to requests or give excuses about the possibility to attend them in the asked terms, or ask new clarifications or give wrong information to block or delay the request's attention. Any behavior that has the effect of not satisfying the request or the systematic delay of its attention could be categorized under this heading.

B. Legal Treatment

486. Since the enactment of Legislative Decree No. 701, refusal to deal has been recognized as an abuse of dominance. The LRCA recognizes this practice as an abuse of dominance under the relative prohibition standard in letter a) of Article 10.2: "To deny to supply or accept offers, of products or services, without justification."

487. Even though INDECOPI has recognized that an undertaking with a dominant position has a right to freely choose who or when it supplies or not, this decision must be supported by an objective and reasonable justification. As in other jurisdictions, the reasoning behind the prohibition relies on the fact that a refusal to deal by an undertaking with a dominant position can affect and distort competition, as it may force one or more competitors to exist in the market or reduce market share, since they rely on the specific product or service supplied by the dominant undertaking to compete.

488. According to the binding precedents issued by INDECOPI under Legislative Decree No. 701 and the LRCA, a refusal to deal will be considered an anticompetitive practice and therefore unlawful, when the following four elements are proven:

(1) The undertaking that refuses to deal has a dominant position on the relevant market.
(2) A refusal to deal has taken place, through the undertakings actions (communications) or elusive responses.
(3) The refusal to deal is not justified by an objective and reasonable justification.
(4) The refusal to deal has an exclusionary effect on competition.

C. Case Law

489. Most of the cases brought to INDECOPI under a "refusal to deal" claim were related to vertical restraints on competition, where the dominant undertaking in the upstream market would refuse to supply a downstream competitor from a subsidiary company. Also, in most cases, claimants alleged the existence of an essential facility controlled by the dominant undertaking, without which a competitor could not enter or stay in the market. Some of the most important cases are detailed below.

490. In *Cab Cable v. Electrocentro S.A.*, Cab Cable (cable television operator) claimed Electrocentro S.A. (electricity distributor) refused to rent its electricity poles, which were essential to provide the wiring required to supply its cable television services. Electrocentro claimed it had an objective and reasonable justification to refuse to rent its poles, as the poles were not set for carrying cable wires in order to comply with the electricity service regulations, among other justifications.

491. In this case, the Commission considered that the technical and commercial justifications alleged by Electrocentro could not justify the refusal. The Commission imposed a fine of 20 UIT (approx. USD 22,000.00) which was later reduced by the Tribunal (court of appeals) to only 5 UIT (approx. USD 5,500.00). Both the Commission and the Tribunal failed to acknowledge the fact that Electrocentro did not compete with Cab Cable and therefore, the practice could not be seen as an exclusionary intent. Moreover, the Tribunal stated that any dominant undertaking in control of an "essential facility" is forced to allow access to any other undertaking if it is technically possible to do so.

492. Likewise, in *Aerocontinente v. BCP*, the first one was accused to refusing to open a current account for the airline company in the city of Puerto Maldonado, despite being the only private bank in the city. The Commission considered that there was no evidence of an anticompetitive practice since Aerocontinente had other alternatives (another bank) to transfer and store its earnings in the city of Puerto Maldonado. The Commission also considered that BCP's conduct was justified since Aerocontinente did not fulfill the requirements and procedures set forth under Peruvian "money laundering" regulations for financial entities.

493. As a result of the appeal filed by Aerocontinente, the Tribunal revoked the Commission's decision and considered that the alternative set forth by it (correspondent account service) was not a perfect substitute to a current account and that this service was essential for Aerocontinente's commercial activities. The Tribunal also considered that the justifications alleged by the BCP were not sufficient, since Aerocontinente's compliance with "money laundering" regulations was not assessed by the BCP in an objective manner.

494. Another example is *FERSIMSAC v. FETRANS*. FERSIMSAC (a rail transport operator) claimed FETRANS (the concessionaire who operates the rail infrastructure to the Machu Picchu ruins who was vertically integrated with PERURAIL, a rail transport operator) refused to rent part of the rolling stock that was given with the concession contract from the Peruvian Government. In this case, the Commission determined that the conduct could not be sanctioned as FETRANS was allowed by the concession contract to rent the entire rolling stock to its own rail transport operator (PERURAIL). The Commission decision was appealed by OSITRAN, the rail infrastructure regulator, acting as a third-interested party.

495. As a result of the appeal, the Tribunal determined that the firm abused its dominant position (being the only infrastructure operator due to the concession) by refusing to rent the rolling stock to any operator other than PERURAIL. The conduct was considered a "strategic entry barrier" since the rolling stock was a "sunk cost" and an "essential facility," due to the investment such assets represented for a new firm. As a behavioral remedy, the Tribunal ordered FETRANS to grant any request by downstream competitors to rent the rolling stock (being used entirely by PERURAIL). Even though it was not ordered, INDECOPI evaluated and almost imposed the vertical separation from FETRANS and PERURAIL, a structural remedy considered necessary to prevent further abuse. Even though this decision was issued in 2007 and later annulled in the judiciary revision due to a lack of due process of law, there is currently an additional operator in the market who entered the market using its own rolling stock, proving the Tribunal inaccuracy.

496. In *AmbevPerú v. Backus & Johnston*, Ambev Perú (brewery) claimed that Backus & Johnston (brewery) denied its incorporation to the Brewers Committee of the National Industries Society (CFC). According to Ambev, Backus denied its participation in the CFC as a strategy to delay or restrict Ambev from entering the Peruvian beer market. This is because only CFC members could participate in a bottle interchangeability system designed to reduce distribution costs, as the CFC had intellectual property rights over the bottle design and trademarks by which beer was sold in Peru. The CFC alleged that Ambev's inclusion was not possible since back then, the company only imported and did not produce any beer. Ambev later withdrew its charges having reached a transaction with Backus. The Commission accepted the withdrawal from Ambev and closed the procedure, since it determined that the alleged conduct did not have any anticompetitive effects. The Commission concluded that Ambev did not need to be a member of the CFC to enter the market, even if this made its commercial operation costlier.

V. Price Squeeze

497. There is no specific prohibition for practices that could be related to the concept of "price squeeze" under the LRCA. INDECOPI has not assessed any practice that could fall under the concept of "price squeeze." Nonetheless, in 2017, OSIPTEL's Tribunal revoked a first instance decision that sanctioned América Móvil Perú S.A.C. (Claro) for price squeeze practices constituting abuse of dominance.

498. In 2012, OSIPTEL's inspection body reported alleged anticompetitive practices executed by Claro to undermine its competitors in the market for prepaid mobile long-distance international calls (LDI). According to the statement of objections, Claro had increased its charges for the provision of LDI wholesale services, while simultaneously lowering its LDI retail prices through three promotional campaigns ('Promoción Prepago 1912', 'Tarifa Especial Números Frecuentes', and 'Triados').

499. Operators requiring LDI wholesale services from Claro were subject to three main charges: (i) a charge for origination of calls in the mobile network; (ii) a charge for access to a payment platform on the mobile network; and (iii) a charge for call termination in destination networks in other countries.

500. OSIPTEL's Collegiate Body conducted a four-step analysis to determine whether Claro had conducted margin squeeze practices:

(1) the first step consisted of analyzing whether the promotional rates allowed Claro a reasonable profit margin;
(2) the second step was to verify if the promotional rates lasted long enough to damage competition;
(3) the third step was to determine if the destinations comprised by the promotional campaigns were particularly relevant in relation to the total traffic generated by Claro's prepaid mobile phones;
(4) finally, the fourth step consisted of evaluating the importance of the traffic generated by the promotional campaigns in relation to Claro's total LDI traffic.

501. Following this test, OSIPTEL's Collegiate Body determined that in the majority of LDI mobile destinations, mainly the most relevant ones, the promotional rates charged by Claro were below the costs considered for the provision of LDI services.

502. Likewise, it determined that the promotional rates were available for a period greater than twelve consecutive months and were significant in Claro's LDI business, thus having a wider anticompetitive potential. Considering this, OSIPTEL's Collegiate Body sanctioned Claro for abuse of dominance in the form of price squeeze.

503. OSIPTEL's Tribunal overruled this decision on appeal by concluding that the Collegiate Body had not carried out an adequate analysis of the variation of the costs charged by Claro during the investigated period. It found out that Claro's costs reasonably varied from destination to destination; thus, the alleged practice had to be analyzed country per country.

504. Unlike the Collegiate Body, the Tribunal considered that such analysis could not be carried out with an estimated average cost by destination blocks since this would not reflect the true cost of LDI call terminations originating in Claro's mobile network. In this sense, Claro's lack of profit margins could not be proven.

505. Furthermore, the Tribunal considered that, rather than the evaluation of the importance of the promotional rates in relation to the operator's traffic, the possible anticompetitive effects of the alleged conduct could be proven by analyzing whether Claro's competitors were in condition to imitate its strategy by offering equal or better rates and generate traffic to their networks.

506. After evaluating the historical conduct of Claro's competitors and determining that their rates were often like Claro's, the Tribunal concluded that there was not enough evidence to demonstrate that Claro had incurred in price squeeze practices in the market for prepaid mobile long-distance international calls (LDI).

VI. Abuse of Legal Procedures or Sham Litigation

A. *Sham Litigation Approach*

507. As it is known, the companies must fulfill the requirements and conditions stated by the legal regulations and obtain authorizations, licenses, concessions, or, in general, the corresponding certifications to initiate operations in the market. While the compliance of the necessary requirements is vital for the operation of such companies to be adequate and secure, the existence of the same legal remedies to question its infringement can be a way of indirectly occasioning incorrect restrictions to the competitive proceeding. As a matter of fact, companies or agents already established can find it attractive or convenient to avoid or delay the entrance of new competitors to the market, opposing themselves to the provision of the permits or certifications mentioned before. In addition, they can also find it useful to legally question the validity of the permits or authorizations already given to the competitors.

508. This way, the competitors can incorrectly avail themselves of the proceedings established in the legal regulations to impede or delay the entrance of competitors or to obstruct their continuity in the market. This type of case will be highly debatable if the one who opposes the entrance of a new company is trying to restrict competition or simply supervising, through the right of action, that the rules of an adequate and secure operation are fulfilled.

B. Legal Treatment

509. In Peru, Sham Litigation is described as an infringement in Article 10 of the LRCA:

> 10.2. The abuse of dominant position in the market may consist on conducts of exclusionary effects such as:
>
> (…)
>
> f) To abuse and reiterate legal or administrative procedure, whose effect is to restrict the competition.
>
> (…)

510. The experience of INDECOPI in this issue circumscribes itself to three cases. However, as it will be seen in the following explanations, the level of study of this figure has gotten deeper each time, contributing an adequate outline of the reach of the prohibited behavior.

511. The prohibition of the abuse of legal procedures allows a healthy equilibrium between the use of the right of action or petition, and the protection of the competition process, becoming a limitation to the behavior of the dominant companies. This way, the companies with dominant position maintain their right of initiation of legal actions but must take care that its exercise does not lead to the constitution of entrance or continuity barriers in the market.

512. After the jurisprudential development that has been given, the elements that characterize this modality of abuse of dominant position are: (i) the repeated use of legal actions against competitors, and (ii) the abusive use of such actions. Being this the last and most difficult element to identify, it has been considered that the abusive character is configured if two conditions are met. First, the absence of an objective basis of a reasonable triumph expectation that sustains the ambition of the agent that initiates or promotes the legal actions must be identified. Only if this is found, second, it must be identified if the procedural activity lacking merit tries to affect the correct functioning of the market, addressing against competitors or seeking the establishment of barriers of entrance (anticompetitive effect).

C. Jurisprudence and INDECOPI's Approach on the Matter

513. The development of the Sham Litigation figure in Peru can be summarized by the following three cases.

514. The first one is *Peruvian Association of Port Operators (APOP) and others v. Pilot Station S.A. (Pilot)*, dated 2007. The pilotage service is offered as support to the ship's captain in maneuvers, complying with the nautical regulations during the realization of operations of berth, casting-off, change of place, turn maneuvers, among others, when the ship uses the port. Given the characteristics of this service, according to the Peruvian regulations, providing it is compulsory for all the ships that go in the main ports of the country. In Peru, this service is provided in free competence conditions.

515. The maritime pilot is the professional who provides this service, for which he has to board the ship and support the operation that is to be performed. For example, if it will berth in one of the ports of the country, he boards the ship and once inside, gives the corresponding instruction so that the ship can go in and get placed in the installations of the port terminal, in adequate and secure conditions.

516. To have the maritime pilot condition, some studies must be followed, and one must count on a specific experience concerning geographical, climate and port location conditions, in which the pilotage service is provided. Additionally, a license (journey licensed captains) provided by the corresponding authority, the Peruvian General Direction of Captaincy and Coastguards (DICAPI) is required. To do this, the number of pilots is reduced for each port, without the possibility of substitution among the number of pilots that provide services in different ports of the country, because of the characteristics of each port.

517. In Peru, the pilotage service was provided through companies especially constituted for the provision of this service, called pilot's administrator companies.

518. Pilot is a pilot's administrator company with a license to provide services in the Callao Port Terminal since December 2000. In 2001, many maritime pilots who worked for Pilot resigned voluntarily from the company, following to integrate other pilots' administrator companies. It must be said that the contracts signed by the referred pilots with Pilot contained an exclusivity clause and were for a determined time, with what, for starters, the resignation to Pilot was not enough to breach the contractual relationship that existed.

519. After the resignations, Pilot initiated a serious judicial and administrative procedures against the pilots who had resigned, many of them relative to the breach of contract. Additionally, Pilot initiated the following actions against Mr. Boggiano:

- Criminal process for the presumed crime against public faith in the mode of falsification of documents before the Ninth Criminal Court of Callao, against the pilot Boggiano Morales.
- Administrative complaint about alleged falsification of document before DICAPI, against the pilot Boggiano Morales.

520. Due to all the legal actions initiated, the APOP and the processed pilots filed a claim before INDECOPI that Pilot was wrongfully using administrative and judicial proceedings to increase the legal entrance barriers to the pilotage service market in the port of Callao, aiming to avoid the maritime pilots who did not work for that company to practice their professional activity freely with other companies of pilotage services, excluding them from the market and/or raising their concurrency costs.

521. Pilot denied the conduct pointing out that a predatory practice of that nature is introduced when the offender's objective is to avoid or delay the entrance of its competitors to the market. In this sense, the mentioned event did not take place in this case as the judicial and administrative procedures were initiated against the pilots who resigned from Pilot for misbehaviors with respect to this company and not against other maritime pilots' administrator companies. Pilot explained that the actions followed against the pilots did not aim to retard the competitors' activities, but looked forward protecting the compliance of a commitment assumed by the dissident pilots (contractual and exclusivity term).

522. The Commission declared that Pilot was responsible for the alleged anti-competitive conduct, commanding it to abstain from developing behaviors contrary to the free market, addressed to punish pilots who left the company and/or avoid access to new pilots to the market. Moreover, it imposed a total of 81.2 UIT between all the offenders, including Pilot, its directors, its director-general manager and managers. For that purpose, the Commission considered that while the legal actions initiated:

> ... had as an aim to avoid the pilots that resigned to Pilot Station to continue performing their pilotage activities (...) that truly had as only purpose to cause a damage to the competitor pilots' administrator companies, trimming the possibility for them of providing themselves with the most important supply to compete in the market, this is, the maritime pilots object of legal actions.[98]

523. With this it was demonstrated that the use of these legal actions did affect the direct competitors of the defendant company, as it meant a delay or obstacle for their access to the market, consolidating as well the dominant position of Pilot Station by other means than economic efficiency.

524. Notwithstanding, the Commission tried to differentiate the correct and legitimate use of the right of action of the anticompetitive practice using the legal actions incorrectly, considering for that distinction, for example, the sense in which the actions initiated by Pilot were solved. In particular, the following was stated:

> This Commission recognizes the legitimate right of every person to demand judicial protection and practice his administrative petition right before the corresponding authorities; however, if the judicial and administrative proceedings placed by the defendant company are belittled (majorly) by the corresponding

98. Resolution No. 037-2005-INDECOPI/CLC, dated Aug. 4, 2005.

authorities, the Commission, in its competence fields, can evaluate and eventually conclude objectively the anticompetitive intention of a company that unnecessarily uses those legal mechanisms with the only purpose of obstructing the access or continuity of the potential or real competitors in the market, and not activating regularly its right of action.

525. Considering the exposed criteria, the Commission concluded that "In this particular case, the analysis of the procedures and proceedings pointed out, it can be concluded that the intention of Pilot Station was to restrict the access to other competitor companies to the services of the pilots that were subject of the administrative and judicial proceedings."

526. In the appeal, the Tribunal confirmed the decision of first instance, including the sanctions imposed.[99] The Tribunal agreed with the Commission by saying that the way in which the actions initiated by Pilot were solved, made it able to deduce the anticompetitive intention of this company:

> From the record it is shown that the authorities in charge of pronouncing themselves about the processes started by Pilot belittled the claims and demands formulated, declaring them inadmissible in some cases due to the lack of competence or unfounded as the infraction alleged did not take place. From this it can be deduced that the aim of Pilot when initiating legal actions against the resigning pilots was to impede them to continue giving their pilotage services through competitor companies.

527. Additionally, the Tribunal stated that the number of actions initiated and the prayer of relief of them were also a relevant matter for the analysis of the illegal character of the use of legal actions: "(…) the number of actions placed by Pilot against each resigning pilot, as well as the prayer of relief in each one of the processes initiated, evidence of the intention of Pilot of impeding the resigning pilots to provide their services through competitor companies."

528. Finally, the Tribunal also emphasized the reduced possibility the competitor companies had if getting alternatives for the habilitated pilots' services to operate in Callao Port and that has stopped providing services with Pilot, with which the strategy developed using legal actions had a major impact over competition:

> Such situation, implied a competition restriction as the pilots' administrator companies' operations depend on their professionals' availability to make the manoeuvres inside the port and considering also that the resigning maritime pilots had been constituted as the only offer available to cover the requirements of the competitor's administrators in the investigation period.

99. Resolution No. 0407-2007/TDC-INDECOPI, dated Mar. 22, 2007.

529. The other case is Peruvian Association of Train Operators (APOFER) v. Ferrocarril Transandino S. A. (FETRANS), PERURAIL S.S. (PERURAIL), Peruval Corp. S.A. (Peruval), and Peruvian Trains & Railways S.A. (PTR), dated 2011.

530. FETRANS is the licensee company of the infrastructure of the South and South-West train, which includes Cusco-Machu Picchu. PERURAIL is the company constituted by FETRANS, according to the foreseen in its license contract, to provide the transport of passengers and charge in the railway service. Peruval and PTR are companies bound to FETRANS and PERURAIL, having shareholders, directors and employees in common.

531. FETRANS, PERURAIL, Peruval and PTR imposed many judicial actions and started many administrative proceedings related to various subjects that were of interest for one or more of them, with one of the following objectives:

(1) Question in the administrative Tribunal, Resolution No. 1122-2007-TDC-INDECOPI, through which it was declared that FETRANS had incurred in abuse of dominant position in the modality of unjustified degrading treatment to rent to FERSIMAC the rolling stock and traction equipment that had been provided as part of the concession of the railway's infrastructure, the same way the non-discrimination duty was imposed so that the referred company provided services in the routes administered by FETRANS, among them, the route Cusco-Machu Picchu.
(2) Request to disregard Supreme Decree No. 031-2007-MTC, which modified the National Railways Regulation, reducing the legal requirements for companies to obtain the rail transport system's operation permit.
(3) Request the modification of the Concession Contract for the Center's Railway signed between Ferrovías Central Andina S.A. and the Ministry of Transport and Communications, with the aim of maintaining the obligation of the concessionaire of not operating the South and South-West Railway, tracks where FETRANS had the concession, and where PERURAIL operated.
(4) Oppose to the permit requests to operate the railway transport in the South-West Train, presented by Andean Railways Corp., Wyoming Railways S.A. and Inca Rail S.A.C.
(5) The adoption of legal actions that would delay the process of modification of the Access Regulations to the railways administered by FETRANS.

532. The questioning in this case was that the defendant companies had abused its right to initiate legal actions, which were only aimed at obstructing or avoiding the competition of railway transport companies in the track Ollantaytambo—Machu Picchu—Hydroelectric Railway (FSO). It was stated that the defendants were part of the same economic group and used the right of action and petition with exclusively predatory means, as they initiated various judicial and administrative proceedings aimed to impede or delay the access of competitor operator companies to the market of railway transport of passengers' services in the FSO, making PERURAIL maintain its position of dominant operator in those tracks. This way, they had incurred in an abuse of dominant position practice for abuse of legal procedures.

533. The defendant denied having incurred in the alleged behavior. PERURAIL and FETRANS stated that they were not part of an economic group. They also said that the claims and petitions laid out in the legal actions questioned by APOFER had full basis and were addressed to defend, in a legitimate way, the business model that was recognized to both companies by the government, as a result of the concession contract for the administration of the FSO given to FETRANS, allowing it to provide railway transportation services to a related company (PERURAIL).

534. Peruval affirmed that its condition of shareholder in FETRANS and PERURAIL did not determine its participation in a combined predatory procedural strategy, even more when it had only placed one judicial action related to the facts regarding the case. Also, Peruval said it did not participate as an economic agent in the relevant market stated by APOFER, for what it could have incurred in an act of abuse of dominant position, and it had not even been evaluated if the only action imposed by Peruval had or not legitimate legal foundation.

535. Finally, PTR affirmed that the corporate link between the defendant companies was inadequate to make it responsible and, as Peruval, it stated that it was not part of the relevant market, so it could not have incurred in acts of abuse of dominant position.

536. The Commission considered that the "(…) retrospective and individual analysis of each legal action was inadequate to determine if the rights of action or petition had been performed to chase other illegal objectives, as the prejudice to free competition. Due to this, the Commission chose a prospective parameter that looks at the motivations that underlie a group or pattern of legal actions."

537. This way, it affirmed that instead of questioning if there is some possible reason in each legal action initiated, we must question if it can be reasonably considered that those actions respond to the interest of protecting the right of the claimant or there is a subsequent or collateral purpose of affecting competition.

538. According to the Commission's analysis, in these cases, it is necessary to evaluate "(…) what is the real motivation of the shareholders," so it said that it must be defined " … if behind the legal processes started there is a real economic profit that justifies incurring in the litigation costs." Additionally, it must be considered that " … the number of legal actions imposed can also be a clarifying element about the motivations of the litigant"; the same way " … the opportunity in which the legal actions are started, the individuals against whom they are addressed and the effects that they can have in the competition," so it allows to verify the anticompetitive intention. Finally, the Commission stated that " … The result of the processes is not decisive to define if the rights of action or petition of an economic agent have been used legitimately."

539. Following the previous ideas, the Commission considered that the legal actions initiated by the defendant, considered as a whole, did not constitute a valid exercise of the rights of action and petition legally recognized, but configured an abuse of legal procedures strategy with the aim of restricting, discouraging, or delaying the entrance of competitors to the railway transport market in the FSO. The Commission noted that it was not necessary to prove that the defendants were part of the same economic group, as the existence of a common and shared interest between them was enough and could be proven by an array of evidence, such as the defendants conduct which was under investigation, as well as documentary evidence which proved they were related.

540. As a result of its analysis, the Commission declared founded the complaint and ordered the defendant to cease the abuse of dominant position through an abuse of legal procedures strategy. Additionally, they were sanctioned with a total fine of 657.5 UIT[100] (approx. USD 850,000).

541. In the appeal, the Tribunal decided to take a different path to the one laid out by the Commission and, instead of identifying the intention of the defendant when starting legal actions, it decided to evaluate each one of the questioned procedures and proceedings, concluding that the denounced had an objective or probable reason that backed up the regular exercise of the rights of petition or action. About that, the Tribunal said that "... before the accusation of a predatory abuse of legal procedures it is essential to analyse if an objective foundation exists, this is, a reasonable expectation of triumph that backs up the claim or claims of the applicant."

542. The Tribunal highlighted as elements to determine the abusive character of the start of the legal actions to identify: "... the absence of objective funding before a plurality of claims or requests deduced, what must be evaluated in a prospective way, this is, in attention to the reasonable expectation of success that these had when the legal processes were initiated."

543. Hence, it considered that the factors evaluated by the Commission were not suitable to reveal in a concluding way the anticompetitive intention. For example, it did not accept the fact that a litigant who tries to satisfy the same interest through initiating various processes or proceedings did not evidence an anticompetitive intention, since "... raising the spectrum of possibilities of achieving a favourable result is a legitimate decision that is outlined in the procedural strategy that each individual adopts." The same way, the Tribunal also discarded the deliberation of the economic costs that occasions a procedure before the economic profit expected (cost of the process before benefits that come from an eventual favorable result), to be an adequate indicator of the anticompetitive motivation, since this deliberation is not only difficult to measure but it gives place to arbitrary decisions of the authorities.

544. On the contrary, the Tribunal considered that if the actions initiated by the defendants had an objective foundation, its qualification as part of a strategy of abusive use of legal proceedings destined to avoid and affect the competition in the

100. Resolution No. 026-2010-INDECOPI/CLC, May 3, 2010.

transport service market in the FSO must be discarded. Hence, it studied each of the legal actions initiated and concluded that they counted with an objective foundation. For example, it considered that FETRANS could have a reasonable expectation of achieving, through the administrative action *(acción contencioso-administrativa)*, that the Tribunal emits a revocation judgment of INDECOPI's decision that declared that it had incurred in abuse of dominant position in the mode of unjustified refusal to rent the rolling stock and traction equipment to FERSIMSAC. The Tribunal understood that while the referred administrative action could delay the possibility of competition in the supplying of railway transport services in the FSO, this effect was admissible as the defendant had an objective foundation to proceed by the administrative jurisdiction.

545. In consequence, the Tribunal revoked the decision issued by the first instance and declared the complaint unfounded.

546. The last and most relevant case is *Cementos Otorongo S.A.C. (COSAC) v. Yura S.A. (Yura)*, part of the Gloria conglomerate, dated 2015.

547. Both companies were competitors in the market for cement production in the south of Peru. According to COSAC, Yura initiated several actions before administrative entities to hinder the construction of a new clinker cement factory by COSAC near Yura's factory. Specifically, COSAC argued that Yura intended to question:

(1) COSAC's construction of a carriageway that would connect the Panamericana Sur highway with COSAC's factory; as Yura had reported to the Regional Government of Arequipa, the National Institute of Culture, in charge of heritage conservation, among other administrative entities, that COSAC allegedly had been carrying out unauthorized constructions;
(2) COSAC's mining activities necessary for the installment of its factory, as Yura had denounced COSAC before the Ministry of Energy and Mines, the Energy and Mining Regulator (OSINERGMIN) and the Environmental Protection Agency (OEFA) for allegedly carrying out mining exploration activities without the corresponding permits and an approved Environmental Impact Assessment report;
(3) The procedure initiated by COSAC to obtain the license required for water usage; since Gloria had allegedly filed a concurrent action to obtain an excluding license in the same area requested by COSAC.

548. To determine whether Yura had developed a sham litigation strategy to undermine COSAC's activities, the Commission established that it had to verify the following two conditions concurrently:

(1) That the agent with a dominant position incurred in a strategy consisting of the abusive and repeated use of legal processes (judicial or administrative).
    For these purposes, the Commission determined that the use of processes will be abusive when it does not have the objective of obtaining a favorable

ruling from the corresponding authorities and, instead, is essentially aimed at injuring the competitors of the dominant agent.

Pursuant to the criteria settled by the Tribunal in the previous case, such a situation can be identified with a throughout analysis of the grounds that support the dominant agent's actions. Other elements that can complement this analysis are the number of processes initiated and the procedural conduct of the dominant agent, which can help to determine if the actions are duly justified; or if, on the contrary, the benefit of taking such actions comes fundamentally from a damage to competition.

(2) That this strategy had the actual or potential effect of harming competition in the relevant market.

549. Considering this, the Commission found that Yura and the Gloria conglomerate had reasonable ground to initiate said actions against COSAC, since, by the time of the issuance of the final resolution, these procedures had already been concluded against COSAC:

(1) for the denounce of COSAC's construction of a carriageway that would connect the Panamericana Sur highway with its factory, the Regional Government of Arequipa determined that COSAC lacked the corresponding authorizations for the development of constructions related to the improvement of the carriageway. Thus, it ordered the immediate work stoppage;
(2) for the denounce of irregularities related to COSAC's mining activities necessary for the installment of its factory, OEFA's Tribunal determined that COSAC lacked the corresponding environmental impact assessment (EIA) to carry out mining exploration activities;
(3) for the alleged obstruction of COSAC's procedures to obtain a water usage license, the Commission determined that even though the Water Authority (ANA) dismissed Yura's actions, Yura had some reasonable ground to claim rights over the water usage license, as a previous decision issued by the Regional Government had recognized Yura's presumed right of priority.

550. Furthermore, the Commission determined that COSAC did not manage to prove that Yura's and Gloria's actions had negative effects on competition. COSAC argued that the questionings significantly delayed its entrance to the market by two years. Nevertheless, the Commission verified that this was the average duration of the procedures, and that Yura's and Gloria's actions had no relevant impact on the terms.

551. Based on these elements, the Commission concluded that Yura and the Gloria conglomerate did not incur in sham litigation practices against COSAC. Resolution No. 29-2015/CLC-INDECOPI was not appealed before the Tribunal.

Chapter 3. Concentrations

552. As will be covered in more detail in Chapter 3 of Part III, from 1997 to 2021, Peru had a merger control regime applicable only to the electricity sector, which was governed by Law No. 26876—Electricity Sector Antimonopoly and Oligopoly Law and its Regulations approved by Supreme Decree N° 017-98-ITINCI. These regulations established that any merger or concentration operation conducted in the electricity market (power transmission, generation, and distribution) required prior approval from INDECOPI as the competition authority. Roughly twenty transactions were notified and assessed while this law was enforceable. Only three of those transactions were approved under certain conditions and none of them were ever denied.

553. On January 7, 2021, Law No. 31112 (hereinafter, the 'Merger Control Law'), a new merger control applicable to all the sectors of the economy was enacted. This law, along with its Regulations approved by Supreme Decree 039-2021-PCM, its Threshold Calculation Guidelines, and Notification Forms, entered into force on June 14, 2021, thus repealing Law No. 26876, and subjecting all the concentration operations meeting the jurisdictional thresholds and having effects in Peru to the prior authorization of INDECOPI.

554. Given the short term in which the current Merger Control Law has been enforceable, there are no decisions reached by the competent bodies in INDECOPI in application of the current and broader merger control regime. It is expected however that, where applicable, the competent bodies will resort to the criteria set in previous cases under the former merger control regime which was exclusive to the electricity market. Being that the case, the following paragraphs describe how the current Merger Control Law is expected to assess each kind of transaction and if possible, reference to case law issued under the former merger control regime.

§1. Horizontal Mergers

555. Under the former merger control regime, a horizontal merger in the electricity market would require prior authorization from INDECOPI if it involved an act of concentration which directly or indirectly involved companies that generated and/or transmitted and/or distributed electric power and jointly or separately, held a market share equal or greater than 15%, prior to the merger or because of it.

556. Under the current merger control regime, there are no special provisions for the evaluation of horizontal mergers, as they are governed by the general rules and the procedure described in Chapter 3 of Part III.

557. It must be noted that out of the three transactions that were authorized under certain conditions during the application of the former merger regime, one involved a pure horizontal merger.

558. This is the case of the concentration operation between INTERCONEXIÓN ELÉCTRICA S.A. E.S.P. and CONSORCIO TRANSMANTARO S.A.—CTM S.A. which were both involved in the power transmission market (the former through REP S.A. and ISA PERU S.A.).

559. By its decision reached in Resolution 081-2006-CLC-INDECOPI, the Commission authorized the operation under the condition that the companies in the economic group led by INTERCONEXIÓN ELÉCTRICA S.A. E.S.P. refrain from exercising their full voting rights in any decision within the Economic Operation Committee of the National Grid (COES). This meant that these companies will only be credited as a single vote, refraining from using any other votes which would be credited to them individually within the COES decision-making processes. The rationale behind this condition was to ensure that the COES operation remains oriented toward the optimal operation of the grid and not individual interests.

560. As a second condition, the economic group led by INTERCONEXIÓN ELÉCTRICA S.A. E.S.P. would refrain from participating in the second call for bids involving the construction and/or expansion of power transmission infrastructure. The rationale behind this condition was to avoid any strategic bidding by the economic group and to create the right incentives to ensure that the group competes with the best possible offer during the first call of the bidding process.

§2. Vertical Mergers

561. Under the former merger control regime, a concentration operation which directly or indirectly involves companies engaging in electric power generation and/or transmission and/or distribution activities that hold a share equal to or greater than 5% of any of the markets involved required prior authorization. The 5% threshold described applied both before the concentration operation or because of it.

562. Under the current merger control regime, there are no special provisions for the evaluation of vertical mergers, as they are governed by the general rules and the procedure described in Chapter 3 of Part III.

563. It must be noted that out of the three transactions that were authorized under certain conditions during the application of the former merger regime, two involved vertical mergers in the markets for power generation and distribution.

564. The first case is the concentration operations between EMPRESA NACIONAL DE ELECTRICIDAD S.A. DE ESPAÑA—ENDESA ESPAÑA and ENERSIS S.A. Through related companies, both companies were involved in the power generation and distribution markets. By the decision reached in Resolution No. 012-1999/CLC-INDECOPI,[101] the Commission authorized the transactions under the condition that one of the generators refrains from casting its vote in any decision

101. Resolution No. 012-1999/CLC-INDECOPI available in Spanish at: https://bit.ly/3dwWEkB.

reached within the board of the COES. As in the previous case, the rationale behind this condition was to avoid the new entity's excessive influence over the decisions reached in the COES.

565. As a second condition, EDELNOR (which held the power distribution concession for the northern part of the capital city of Lima) was to carry out private bidding processes for its power requirements. The rationale behind this condition was to ensure that the distribution concessionaire would not acquire its power requirements exclusively from its related generators (EDEGEL, ETEVENSA and EEPSA) or somehow show some preference toward them, guaranteeing competition in the supply of power for distribution.

566. A more recent decision involved the concentration operation between CHINA YANGTZE POWER INTERNATIONAL CO. LIMITED (a state-owned Chinese power generator) and SEMPRA AMERICAS BERMUDA LTD., as well as PERUVIAN OPPORTUNITY COMPANY S.A.C. (companies involved in the power generation and distribution markets). The former would acquire the total shares of SEMPRA AMERICAS BERMUDA LTD. and 50% of the shares of PERUVIAN OPPORTUNITY COMPANY S.A.C.

567. By the decision reached in Resolution No. 007-2020/CLC-INDECOPI,[102] the Commission authorized the transaction under the condition that LUZ DEL SUR (which held the power distribution concession for the southern part of the capital city of Lima) was to carry out private bidding processes for its power requirements. The rationale behind this condition was to ensure that the distribution concessionaire would not acquire its power requirements exclusively from its related generators or somehow show some preference toward them, guaranteeing competition in the supply of power for distribution.

§3. Market/Product Extension Mergers

568. Under the former merger control regime there were no special provisions regarding the evaluation of market/product extension mergers, considering this regime applied only to the electricity market (i.e., power generation, transmission, and distribution). Under the current merger control regime, there are no special provisions for the evaluation of market/product extension mergers, as they are governed by the general rules and the procedure described in Chapter 3 of Part III.

§4. Pure Conglomerate mergers

569. Under the current merger control regime, there are no special provisions for the evaluation of pure conglomerate mergers, as they are governed by the general rules and the procedure described in Chapter 3 of Part III. It must be noted that pure

102. Resolution No. 007-2020/CLC-INDECOPI available in Spanish at: https://bit.ly/3qCQx3t.

conglomerate mergers are not exempt from prior authorization if the transaction involved falls within the applicable thresholds and the scope of the Merger Control Law. During the review procedure, the undertakings requesting authorization may present the case that the transaction granting "control" does not have anticompetitive effects on the relevant market and therefore should be authorized unconditionally.

§5. Joint Ventures

570. Under both the former and current merger control regimes, there are no special provisions for the evaluation of joint ventures. Given that joint ventures confer control over a company, the celebration of these types of agreements is considered a merger and is subject to merger control under the current merger control regime.

Part III. Administrative Procedure

Chapter 1. Administrative Investigations Before the Antitrust Authority

§1. Initiative

I. General Sector Inquiries

571. According to the LRCA and the current structure of INDECOPI, the NDC is the technical autonomous body which performs the task of an instructor of the investigation and punishment procedure of anticompetitive conducts; and issues an opinion on the existence of the offending conduct.

572. Investigations can be initiated ex officio or based on complaints presented by competitors or any party with interest. The NDC's Director decides as to whether it will initiate an investigation or admit the complaint.

573. The infringement procedure may be initiated when the reported conduct is being performed, when there is a threat of it and even when its effects have already stopped.

574. According to the amendments to Articles 14 and 15 of the LRCA by Legislative Decree No. 1205 in September 2015, the Commission has the power of authority to suggest, exhort or recommend public administration entities the implementation of measures that re-establish or promote competition, such as the elimination of bureaucratic entry barriers or the application of regulation to a given market where competition is not feasible, among others. The President of INDECOPI's Board of Directors will submit said recommendations to the public entities, which are required to provide a statement with their comments within ninety working days. These recommendations are also notified to the Council of Ministers Presidency and the Ministry of Economy.

575. The NDC has the power to conduct preliminary investigations in any sector or market (whether it involves public administration entities or only private sector agents). Moreover, the recent amendment commented above introduced letter g) to the list of powers the NDC has in Article 15 of the LRCA, stating that it has the power to conduct studies and publish reports, including any investigation or inquiry activity needed to propose the Commission the actions needed to execute the mandate detailed above.

II. Ex Officio Investigations

576. According to Article 15 of the LRCA, if the NDC suspects an infringement of the competition rules, it may commence a preliminary investigation in the market. The basis for suspected infringements could be provided by informal complaints, market analyses, sudden price changes, information from the media or other indicators of market irregularity. The authority's first step in relation to the company could be to issue a request for information or carry out a dawn raid.

577. After that, the NDC is authorized to initiate the procedure ex officio for investigating and punishing anticompetitive conducts.

578. Based on the amendments introduced by Legislative Decree No. 1510 and Law No. 31112, the NDC has the power to decide whether to initiate a procedure or not, if it considers that the conduct or practice which is subject to the "relative prohibition" (i.e., "Rule of Reason") is not capable of significatively affecting competition. In this case, the NDC may impose actions or measures that reinstate or promote competition.

III. Complaints

579. Article 15 of the LRCA also established that in case of a complaint, the NDC decides whether to admit a complaint and initiate a procedure on its basis, being also entitled to declare the complaint inadmissible.

580. When a complaint is received, the NDC will determine if it is sufficiently founded to warrant an investigation. Article 18 of the LRCA established that in the trilateral procedure, the complainant is a collaborator in the investigation procedure, while the NDC preserves the power to initiate and conduct the procedure.

581. Article 19 of the LRCA states that the complaint charging the anticompetitive conducts shall contain:

(a) Name, denomination or legal name of the complainant, its domicile and respective powers, if applicable.
(b) Reasonable evidences of the alleged existence of one or more anticompetitive conducts.
(c) Identification of the alleged responsible, as far as it is possible.
(d) The expenses vouchers of procedure fees for infringement procedure. These procedure fees are exempted from the limit, regarding the established amount in the General Administrative Procedure Law—Law No. 27444.

582. Once the complaint is filed and prior to the NDC's decision of whether to admit the complaint, the NDC may carry out its investigation in order to identify reasonable evidence of anticompetitive conducts. These prior proceedings shall be developed in no more than forty-five working days from the filing date of the complaint.

583. After that, the NDC shall decide on the admissibility of a complaint after verifying the compliance of the legal requirements demanded, the jurisdiction of the Commission and the existence of reasonable evidence of infringement to this law.

§2. Powers

I. Requests for Information

584. According to Articles 15.2 and 15.3 of the LRCA, the NDC has the authority to request all necessary information from undertakings, regarding current investigation procedures initiated by a party's request or ex officio:

> 15.2. The NDC has the following functions:
>
> (a) To execute preliminary investigations;
> (b) To initiate ex officio the procedure for investigating and punishing anticompetitive conducts.
>
> (...)
>
> 15.3. For the development of its investigations, the Technical Secretariat is empowered to:
>
> (a) Demand individuals, business associations and autonomous properties, to exhibit all kind of documents, including accounting and corporate books, payment vouchers, internal and external correspondence and magnetic records including, in this case, the needed programs for its reading; as well as to request information regarding the organization, its businesses, the shareholders and the ownership structure of firms.
> (b) Summon or examine, through the officers assigned for such purpose, the individuals under investigation or its representatives, employees, officers, advisors and third parties, using technical resources it deems necessary to generate a complete and accurate record of its statements, being entitled to use magnetic tape recordings in video, compact disc or any other electronic instrument.
> (c) To conduct dawn raids, with or without prior notification, at the premises of the natural or legal person, business associations and autonomous properties, and examine books, records, documents and goods, being entitled to check on the development of the production processes and take the statement of the persons found at the premise. In the dawn raid may take copies of physical files, magnetic or electronic, as well as any document that

is deemed relevant or taking photographs or filming as may be necessary... To access such premises, police support may be requested.

(...)

585. According to Article 15.3, to carry out its investigations, the NDC has the power to require the exhibition of any type of document from both natural and legal persons, without judicial authorization. Moreover, the NDC has the power to summon and question any officer or official representative—regardless of rank or position—of any legal person or entity, requesting all cooperation deemed necessary. This will not require any previous judicial authorization.

586. Information disclosure under this authority will be mandatory, unless the requested information is considered confidential or personal, according to the fundamental rights established in the Peruvian Constitution. In these exceptional cases, a judicial authorization will be necessary prior to the request.

587. The NDC has the power to carry out dawn raids to the premises or offices of any of the undertakings, associations of undertakings, or natural persons. These dawn raids do not require prior notice of any kind. No special procedure is required to carry out these dawn raids; however, it has been a common practice by the NDC to submit a letter or notification to the undertaking, explaining its powers to conduct the dawn raid and the existence of an ongoing investigation.

588. If a party under investigation submits false information, hides information, alters information, destroys information or is reluctant to submit information, a fine of up to 1000 UIT (Approx. USD 1.07 million) will be imposed according to Article 43.7 of the LRCA. According to Article 37 of the LRCA, this fine can be appealed.

589. During the dawn raid, the information request procedure and the entire administrative procedure, a party under investigation has a right against self-incrimination.

II. Investigating and Search Powers

590. As mentioned above, Article 15.3 of the LRCA grants the NDC powers to conduct dawn raids in the offices and premises of the party under investigation.

591. In 2020, INDECOPI published the Dawn Raids Guidelines with the purpose of providing transparency and defining the scope of action of the NDC in the context of a dawn raid, describing its main characteristics and particularities, as well as the rights and obligations of the economic agents who are the subject to these proceedings.

592. Before the NDC decides to conduct a dawn raid, the following parameters are to be considered: (i) a material parameter that consists of reasonable evidence obtained by the NDC that indicates the possible commission of such anticompetitive offenses; and (ii) a formal parameter, that implies that the representatives of the authority must previously deliver the so-called dawn raid decision, which is a document that contains the written authorization by the NDC in order to conduct such proceeding.

593. As a rule, these dawn raids are carried out without prior notification after the officers in charge receive the "dawn raid decision." The undertaking under investigation will be notified with a letter that comprises the special powers from the NDC during the initiation of the dawn raids.

594. The dawn raid decision must contain several elements and requirements, with the following being the most important:

(a) A general description of the conduct under investigation and the alleged affected market.
(b) The name of the undertaking under investigation.
(c) The identification of the premise in which the dawn raid will be developed (considering that the company could have several premises).
(d) The identification of the inspectors in charge of the dawn raid.
(e) The date of the beginning of the dawn raid.
(f) The legal basis of the dawn raid powers of the authority, as well as the documents and information that is aimed to be obtained and/or evaluated.
(g) The duties and obligations of the investigated company, including the sanctions and consequences to possible infringement scenarios.
(h) The object and purpose of the dawn raid.

595. Given that the dawn raid powers granted by the legal framework entail a limitation of the rights of the parties under investigation, these are mandated to collaborate with the entities and assume the consequences derived from such supervisory action, known as the "collaboration duty." This duty implies that the undertaking under investigation has to provide access and facilities to: (i) its commercial premises; (ii) any information deemed relevant to the object of the investigation; and (iii) the shooting of pictures and footage. The undertaking under investigation must also facilitate interviews with its officers or representatives.

596. Inspectors are entitled to review and obtain copies of any information considered relevant to the investigation, regardless of the storage medium (physical, digital, etc.). For such purposes, they will be able to access any book, document, desktop computers, servers, tablets and any other physical or electronic storage media located at the premise of the company under the dawn raid, including all the emails and electronic files located in the accounts of the representatives and employees of the company, as well as information stored in remote sources.

597. The undertakings under investigation will inform the inspectors of any information that falls outside the object of the investigation, which may include intimate or personal information, as well as that protected by legal privileges. This information shall not be collected. During the dawn raid, the NDC might extend or vary the object of the investigation in case it gathers or identifies information related to possible facts or infringements different from those contained in the dawn raid decision. This possibility will be informed to the investigated companies through the dawn raid decision.

598. In case original or personal documents (e.g., personal emails) are mixed in in the computers and similar equipment of the companies, and it is not possible to easily separate such information during the short term of the raid, the company has the possibility to carry out this task. In these cases, the inspectors will also be empowered to preliminarily verify the content of such documents, with the purpose of validating whether it is indeed intimate or irrelevant information for the investigation.

599. The officials of the NDC should comply with a strict duty of secrecy and confidentiality regarding the information obtained during the dawn raid, finding themselves prevented from disclosing the information under the risk of being held administratively liable.

600. Interviews with officers, employees, or official representatives, may be conducted by the NDC during the dawn raids. Usually, these will be conducted at the same time. If the requested person is not available for the interview, this may be rescheduled for later, if the NDC deems it necessary for the investigation purposes. It is important to emphasize that any obstruction or lack of cooperation with the NDC to provide information may be considered an infraction and be subject to a fine.

601. In the context of a dawn raid, parties can request professional advice if they consider it appropriate, as stated in Section 242.6 of Law No. 27444. This right is usually reflected in the presence of a lawyer during the proceedings, there to accompany the inspectors, make observations, and review the content of the dawn raid records at the end of it. However, the presence of such legal counsel is not an essential requirement to begin the dawn raid, nor its absence can condition the development of the dawn raid.

602. Acts that suppose any type of obstruction or non-compliance during a dawn raid are susceptible of a sanction with fines up to 1,000 UIT according to Article 43.7 of the LRCA.[103] These conducts will be evaluated in the corresponding administrative sanctioning procedure, allowing the company to exercise its right of defense and present the allegations and supporting material they deem appropriate.

603. Among others, the following conducts qualify as obstruction cases:

(a) Denying or unreasonably obstructing the access of inspectors to the premises of the company (or to certain sources of information).

103. Approx. USD 1.07 million.

(b) Erroneously identifying those employees responsible for the areas under investigation (or their respective offices), as well as providing inaccurate information about their presence or the location of certain sources of information.
(c) Not presenting (or doing so incompletely) the goods, documents or files requested by the inspectors.
(d) Providing false or inaccurate information (either through statements and/or documents), as well as altering, hiding, or destroying the items or files under the dawn raid.
(e) Obstructing the exercise of the functions of the inspectors through violence or threats.
(f) Denying answering the questions asked by the inspectors, if these do not imply an admission of guilt from the investigated parties.
(g) Not complying with the measures of non-mobilizations ordered by the Commission.

604. Finally, the information obtained by the NDC that is relevant to the investigation will be analyzed to determine whether it is appropriate to initiate a sanctioning administrative procedure against the investigated company. If that is the case, this information will be incorporated into the case file, so that the parties are able to enforce their right of defense and present the exculpatory evidence that they consider relevant.

III. Cooperation with Other State Institutions

605. Cooperation between all public administration entities is regulated under Article 76 of the General Administrative Procedure Law—Law No. 27444. This article forces all public administration entities to share information between them for investigation purposes.

606. Even when this legal rule is in place, there are several different degrees of cooperation between public entities. As an example, OSINERGMIN (National Energy and Mining Private Investment Supervisor) has an agreement with INDECOPI to provide information related to the energy and mining markets.

607. In the same way, INDECOPI has entered into a series of agreements with other Latin-American competition agencies, such as Chile's FNE (Fiscalía Nacional Económica) and Colombia's SIC (Superintendencia de Industria y Comercio). These agreements seek to allow information exchange between competition agencies regarding relevant aspects to INDECOPI's own investigations.

§3. Right of Defense

I. Content and Notification of Opening Decisions

608. According to Article 21 of the LRCA, the NDC's opening decision shall include:

(1) the identification of an economic Agent or Agents who are charged with the alleged offense;
(2) a concise statement of the facts underlying the establishment of the procedure, the legal definition of the alleged offense and, where appropriate, all the sanctions that may correspond;
(3) the identification of the Commission as the authority with jurisdiction over the case and the legal basis for its powers; and,
(4) the right the investigated party has to present the case for the defense and the deadline to do so.

609. The decision of initiation of procedure shall be informed to the Commission in a period of no more than five working days. The parties under investigation and those who filed the complaint will also be notified within this period. The decision declaring that a complaint is inadmissible can be appealed before the Tribunal within a period of fifteen working days.

610. Once the complaint has been admitted, the NDC may choose to publish a brief note on its subject matter, so that anyone with legitimate interest may request to be part of the procedure or simply provide useful information for the investigation. Such note shall be published in INDECOPI's webpage, in the Official Gazette and in any widely circulated newspaper in the national territory.

611. According to the Peruvian law, the sanctioning procedure may be initiated when the denounced behavior is on course, when there is an existent threat of it taking place, and even when its effects have already ceased.

II. The Proceedings: Hearings, Access to File, Briefs

612. The defendant or defendants shall answer the charges in the decision of initiation of procedure within a period of thirty working days, submitting the arguments they deem convenient and providing the corresponding evidence.

613. During this period, other parties with legitimate interest may intervene in the procedure, expressing their arguments and providing relevant evidence, subject to fulfillment of the requirements for filing a complaint of a party.

614. During the administrative sanctioning procedure, only those who are considered "parties" in the procedure (the undertaking under investigation, the claimant or any other third party with legitimate interest which has been previously credited as a party in the procedure) have the right to access the case file, its content and request information regarding the status of the procedure.

615. While this is the case for most of the information on the case file, access to information declared Confidential by the Commission will be reserved for the party that owns said information, authorized officials from the Commission or the NDC, as well as any other party under investigation that requires it to fully exercise its right of defense.

616. Once the parties under investigation have filed their respective defense arguments, the evidence phase will start, in which the parties may file additional arguments and evidence. The evidence phase will last up to seven months. The following evidence may be put forward:

(a) Documents.
(b) Party's statements.
(c) Testimonies.
(d) Dawn Raids.
(e) Expertise.
(f) Other evidences if in the opinion of the Technical Secretariat are needed to clarify the facts alleged or charged.

617. The cost of the evidence shall be borne by the person who offered it. The costs of those ordered by the authority may be distributed between the accused and who filed the complaint, if any, when the procedure is finished and depending on its outcome.

618. The Director of the NDC has the power to use its discretion to determine whether any information or evidence provided by any party is manifestly irrelevant or unnecessary to determine the existence of the anticompetitive conduct.

619. After the evidence phase has concluded, the NDC will inform to the parties stating that from that point on, any information, argument or evidence presented will not be considered.

620. During the evidence phase or after its conclusion, the NDC may be confronted with new information which alters the grounds or conclusions in the decision that contains the charges under investigation (e.g., evidence of a previously unidentified anticompetitive conduct). The NDC has the power to alter its initial decision to incorporate these new findings. This decision will replace the former and be duly notified to the parties, initiating a new evidence phase.

III. Statement of Objections

621. Within thirty working days of the conclusion of the evidence phase, the NDC will produce its "Technical Report" containing the statement of objections against the parties under investigation. According to Article 36 of the LRCA the report will cover the following:

- Proven facts.
- The existence of the administrative infringement.
- The identification of those responsible.
- The fines proposed.
- The corrective measures proposed.

622. Should the NDC find there are no grounds to conclude the anticompetitive conduct existed or that the parties under investigation can be held accountable for it, it will propose the Commission to rule that no infringement to the LRCA took place.

623. Parties will be notified with the Technical Report and given a thirty working days period to present their counterarguments and or request to address the Commission in a final hearing.

624. Under its sole discretion, the Commission may consider further evidence is required to reach its decision and will exceptionally open a second evidence phase for thirty working days. Parties can present additional arguments and/or evidence during this phase.

IV. Final Hearing and Decision

625. Under its sole discretion, the Commission may request or grant a final hearing in which parties are expected to present the case for the defense and address the recommendations put forth in the NDC's Technical Report. The NDC has no role in this hearing.

626. If a second evidence phase is opened by the Commission, the Commission may request a second hearing.

627. The parties may present their final allegations within ten working days after both the first and second hearing took place. No additional evidence can be filled after these final allegations.

628. The Commission must issue its final decision on the case within sixty working days from the deadline parties had to present their final allegations.

§4. Appeal to the Competition Tribunal

629. The Commission's final decision could be appealed by the looser party or by third parties with a legitimate interest who have attended to the procedure before the Tribunal within fifteen working days. According to Article 40 of the LRCA, the NDC may appeal the decision to exonerate the investigated parties, as well as the fine imposed.

630. The parties interested in determining the existence of an infringing conduct and the imposition of a penalty may only appeal the final decision when it has acquitted the accused party. Based on the *reformatio in peius* principle, The Tribunal cannot increase the amount of the fines imposed by the Commission.

631. The appeal does not suspend the effects of the decision being appealed, unless otherwise stated by the authority granting the appeal (the NDC or the Commission, depending on whose decision is being challenged).

632. The appeal process will not last more than a hundred and twenty working days. The Tribunal's decision will be notified to the parties involved in the procedure and to any other party credited as such during the procedure.

633. At its sole discretion, the Tribunal shall grant or request a hearing in which parties can present their case. After the hearing, parties are given five working days to present their final allegations. Arguments or evidence presented once this period has concluded will not be taken into consideration by the Tribunal.

634. Acts that render the continuation of the procedure impossible, acts that can affect the ability of the defendant to exercise its right of defense or those that can inflict irreparable damage to rights or legitimate interests can also be appealed.

Chapter 2. Voluntary Notifications and Clearance Decisions

635. Aside from voluntary notifications under the Merger Control regime, which is described in the following chapter, there are no other voluntary notifications that any undertaking or party can file or submit regarding the application of the LRCA.

Chapter 3. Merger Control

§1. Pre-merger Filing Obligations

I. Criteria and Thresholds

636. From 1997 to 2021, Peru had a merger control regime applicable only to the electricity sector, which was governed by Law No. 26876—Electricity Sector Antimonopoly and Oligopoly Law and its Regulations approved by Supreme Decree N° 017-98-ITINCI. These regulations established that any merger or concentration procedure conducted in the electricity market (power transmission, generation, and distribution) required the prior approval from INDECOPI as the competition authority. Roughly twenty transactions were notified and assessed while this law was enforceable. Only three of those transactions were approved with conditions and none of them were denied.

637. On January 7, 2021, Law No. 31112 (hereinafter, the "Merger Control Law"), a new merger control applicable to all the sectors of the economy was enacted. This Law, along with its Regulations, approved by Supreme Decree 039-2021-PCM, its Threshold Calculation Guidelines, and Notification Forms, entered into force on June 14, 2021, thus repealing Law No. 26876, and subjecting all the concentration operations meeting the jurisdictional thresholds and having effects in Peru to the prior authorization of INDECOPI.

638. In this context, the Merger Control Law defines "control" as the possibility of exerting a decisive and continuous influence over an economic agent through rights of ownership or use of all or part of a company's assets, or rights or contracts that allow a decisive and continuous influence on the structure, deliberations, or decisions of a company's bodies, determining, either directly or indirectly, the competitive strategy of a firm.

639. The Merger Control Law defines concentration operations as any act or operation that involves a transfer or change in control of a company or part of it. The term "permanent" has been removed from the definition of a concentration act in the new law. Nonetheless, considering the regulations, the change of control should be intended to be permanent for an operation to qualify as a concentration.

640. According to the Merger Control Law and its Regulations, the following four types of transactions will typically fall within the concept of "concentrations":

(a) a merger;
(b) the formation of a joint venture which is intended to be permanent and fully functional;
(c) the direct or indirect acquisition of control over other companies through different means, such as the acquisition of shares, participations, or through any other contract or legal figure that confers direct or indirect control of a company; and

(d) the acquisition of productive assets operative in the past twelve months with the following characteristics:
   - to which a defined income volume is attributable;
   - that can reinforce or increase the market share of the acquirer; and
   - that have generated income during the year prior to notification.

641. On the other hand, the Merger Control Law contains the following list of transactions that will not be considered as "concentration operations" subject to prior notification:

- the corporate growth of an economic agent as a result of operations carried out exclusively within the same economic group;
- the internal corporate growth of an economic agent, regardless of whether it takes place through own investment or with resources of third parties that do not participate in the market;
- the corporate growth of an economic agent that does not produce effects in the markets within the domestic territory, either in whole or in part;
- control acquired over an economic agent because of a temporary mandate conferred by law relating to the forfeiture or denunciation of a concession, asset restructuring, insolvency, creditors' agreement, or other similar procedure; and
- the temporary holding by credit, financial, insurance or capital market institutions of stocks or shares acquired for the purpose of resale, provided that no voting rights are exercised to determine the competitive behavior of that undertaking.

642. Successive transactions by the same parties within a period of two years are considered as a single notifiable transaction if it creates a concentration. The transaction must be notified prior to the implementation of the last transaction.

643. The criteria to which "concentration operations" will be reviewed intends to determine if they would create a significant restriction to competition on the markets involved. According to Article 7 of the Merger Control Law, the Competition Commission will evaluate the following aspects to conduct its impact assessment:

- market structure;
- current or potential competition;
- the evolution of supply and demand;
- distribution or commercialization sources;
- legal barriers and other kinds of barriers (technological, horizontal or vertical restrictions) for market entrance;
- the economic and financial power of the involved agents;
- the creation or strengthening of a dominant position;
- the production of economic efficiencies.

644. For economic efficiencies to be taken into consideration, they must be productive, allocative, or innovative efficiencies that meet the following requirements:

– they must be proven by the applicant economic operators;
– they must be inherent in the concentration;
– they must be aimed at outweighing identified restrictive effects on competition and improving consumer welfare;
– they must be transferable to the consumer; and
– they must be verifiable by the authority.

645. According to Article 6 of the Merger Control Law, transactions that involve a transfer or change in the control of an economic agent must obtain a prior merger authorization by INDECOPI if they meet or exceed the following jurisdictional thresholds:

(i) The total sum of the value of annual sales or gross income or the value of the assets in the country of the companies involved in the concentration during the fiscal year prior to notification should be equal to or greater than 118,000 UIT, approximately USD 141 million.
(ii) The value of the annual sales or gross income or the value of the assets in the country of at least two of the companies involved in the concentration during the fiscal year prior to notification should be each equal to or greater than 18,000 UIT, approximately USD 21.5 million.

646. There are no special jurisdictional thresholds applicable to specific sectors.

647. It must be mentioned that INDECOPI has the power to initiate ex officio investigations and review closed operations that fall below those thresholds, when the authority considers they could potentially restrict competition because of:

(i) Transactions in concentrated markets.
(ii) Acquisition of competitors with small market participation and growth potential.
(iii) Acquisition of competitors that have recently entered the market.
(iv) Successive acquisition of competitors in the market.
(v) Other operations with similar effects.

648. Concentrations involving first landing economic agents that had no income in the country during the previous year cannot be reviewed. INDECOPI's power is subject to a time limit of one year from the closing of the operation. INDECOPI may force the sale of the acquired shares/assets, among other remedies because of the exercise of its ex officio power to review closed transactions. However, agents can present a voluntary notification when the thresholds are not met.

649. Lastly, the Merger Control Law forbids issues which are not related to competition to be considered as part of the assessment of a concentration. The Merger Control Law states that INDECOPI will not consider issues which are not related to the merger regime's purpose, which is related to economic efficiency and consumer welfare.

II. Turnover Calculation

650. In relation to threshold calculation, the Merger Control Act Regulations establish that Depending on the operation, threshold calculation considers the following agents' total annual gross sales or revenue (annual turnover) or asset book value in Peru during the previous fiscal year:

(1) For the case of mergers and constitution of joint ventures: Both economic agents and their economic groups.
(2) For the case of acquisition of control over another economic agent: Acquiring agent and its economic group, and the target and the agents it controls.
(3) For the case of acquisition of an operative productive asset: Acquiring agent and its economic group, and sales or revenue attributable to the acquired asset or its book value.

651. Following along, in May 2021, INDECOPI's Antitrust Commission published the Threshold Calculation Guidelines ("*Lineamientos para el cálculo de umbrales de notificación*"). According to the Guidelines, either the income or asset value thresholds will be considered individually.

652. Regarding income, the calculations shall include revenue coming from the operations carried out by the concentrating parties during their ordinary course of business. Only the sale of products to clients located in Peru and services provided to clients located in Peru is to be considered. Threshold calculation excludes income from transactions outside the usual course of business, taxes, and sales within the same economic group.

653. Regarding assets, the calculations shall consider the book value of all assets (tangible and intangible) located in Peru, except those that were not located in the country during the previous year. Threshold calculation excludes assets located in Peru for which more than 50% of the income generated corresponds to sales to foreign customers.

654. It must be considered that, according to the Thresholds Calculation Guidelines, the relevant exchange rate to be used for threshold calculations must be the average exchange rate of the last twelve months prior to the notification, as determined by the Peruvian Central Bank.

655. The Merger Control Law considers the sales volume or asset value of the economic agents involved in the merger transaction. According to the type of transaction, the income or asset values considered should include those of the agent involved and its economic group. The Thresholds Calculation Guidelines state that to identify an economic group the definitions of the law and previous case law should be considered. Therefore, if an economic agent holds sole or joint control of another company all the income or asset value of the controlled company should be counted, regardless of the number of shares such economic agent could have over the company.

656. Finally, regarding transactions involving a company in which the State is a shareholder, the Thresholds Calculation Guidelines state that income or assets value should consider all companies belonging to the same decision unit. Since in Peru, state-owned companies are controlled by FONAFE (*Fondo Nacional de Financiamiento de la Actividad Empresarial del Estado*), all state-owned companies will be considered as part of the same decision unit.

III. Market Share Calculation

657. As stated above, the Merger Control Law does not provide a market share jurisdictional threshold. This constitutes a change from the previous merger control regime which was applicable only to the electricity sector. Under the previous regime, horizontal concentrations between companies that generated, transmitted and/or distributed electric power held a market share equal to or greater than 15% either directly or indirectly, jointly, or separately required notification.

IV. Other Relevant Notions

658. Under the Merger Control Law, there are no provisions that allow a transaction to take place before clearance.

659. Failure to notify a concentration operation is sanctionable with a fine of up to 500 Tax Units (approx. USD 596,000 for 2021). Gun jumping, consisting of the execution of a transaction before obtaining clearance, is sanctionable with a fine of up to 1,000 Tax Units (approx. USD 1.1 million for 2021). Likewise, the execution of a transaction that was prohibited by INDECOPI is sanctionable with a fine of up to 12% of the sales of the offender or its economic group.

§2. Structure of Proceedings

I. Preliminary Assessment and Full Investigation

660. According to Article 17 of the Merger Control Law, undertakings involved in the concentration operation may jointly or individually request the non-binding opinion of the NDC regarding the application of the merger control regime to the operation, whether it falls within the scope of the law, which information must be submitted with their application, among other related aspects. The opinion of the NDC does not bind the Commission's decisions in any way.

661. In June 2021, the Commission approved and published the Ordinary Notification Form and the Simplified Notification Form, which contain the necessary background information to assess the concentration and its possible effects of the operation on competition in the markets involved.

662. The latter is designed for concentrations deemed to be less likely to produce any significant restrictions to competition. Transactions which are eligible for the simplified notification comprise the following:

– non-overlap concentrations: the economic agents involved in the concentration transaction or their economic groups do not carry out economic activities in the same product market and in the same geographic market; or, they do not participate in the same production or value chain; or
– change from joint to single control: the concentration transaction generates that an economic agent acquires exclusive control of another economic agent over which it already has control.

663. It must be noted that the submission of a simplified form is not part of a fast-track procedure, as it only requires a less burdensome notification form with no changes in the terms for the review of the concentrations. In that sense, the competent body in INDECOPI will assess the effects of the concentration operation following the criteria set in Article 7 of the Merger Control Law to identify whether it produces a significant restriction of competition in the markets involved, regardless of the form used in the application.

II. Time Framework

664. The Merger Control Law establishes a two-phase review procedure. The first stage is the notification phase: after the submission, the NDC assesses the information filed by the parties to determine whether all the requirements have been met in a period of ten working days. If any requirement is missing, an additional ten working day period is granted to the parties for rectification, after which the NDC declares the application admissible or inadmissible within a period of five working days.

665. Once the notification is admitted, Phase I involves the Commission's evaluation as to whether the concentration falls within the scope of the law, as well as whether it raises serious competition concerns. This stage lasts a maximum of thirty working days. If the Commission does not find any serious competition concerns or finds that the transaction does not fall within the scope of the law, the transaction is approved. However, if serious competition concerns arise from the Commission's evaluation, the assessment moves on to Phase II. Both decisions must be notified to the parties.

666. If the Commission does not issue a decision within the respective period, the concentration is automatically authorized because of the application of positive administrative silence.

667. Phase II lasts a maximum of ninety working days. It starts once the Commission has notified the parties that the transaction has moved on to the next stage of evaluation and a summary of the concentration has been made public to allow third parties to present relevant information. This period may be extended for an additional thirty working days, with due justification by the authority for such extension. This period could also be extended for fifteen additional working days if the parties involved require hearings.

668. The Commission can suspend the procedure if the parties have proposed commitments to analyze them, whether in Phase I or Phase II.

669. Under the Merger Control Law, the approximate term of the procedure is a hundred and ninety working days at the Commission level (first instance), and a hundred and fifteen working days on appeal.

III. Right of Defense

670. Under the Merger Control Law, the burden of proof regarding the anticompetitive impact of the concentration operation is placed on the competent body of INDECOPI. The undertakings requesting authorization must provide evidence of the nature, scope, and probability of the transaction's economic efficiencies.

671. During the review procedure, the undertakings requesting authorization may present their case to the competent body of INDECOPI, including offering measures and commitments which aim to avoid or mitigate the anticompetitive effects the concentration operation might have.

672. Moreover, according to Article 24 of the Merger Control Law, the undertakings requesting authorization can request a hearing at any phase of the review. As a result, the timeframe for authorization may be extended for an additional fifteen working days.

673. If the authorization request is denied or conditioned, the undertakings requesting authorization can appeal the Commission's decision within fifteen working days after notification. The Tribunal will review the appeal in a maximum of ninety working days. A judicial review is also possible under the same rules that apply to any other decision reached by the Tribunal.

§3. Clearance and Conditional Clearance

I. Conditions and Undertakings

A. Content

674. Clearance is given with the decision of the Commission or if said is subjected to an appeal, the decision of the Tribunal. The procedure may also end with an authorization if the "positive administrative silence" applies, provided that the competent body has exceeded the respective term without reaching a decision.

675. As part of its decision, the Commission may (i) deny admission of the filing, if the merger is not within the scope of application of the act, (ii) authorize the concentration operation, (iii) authorize the concentration operation under certain commitments or conditions, or (iv) prohibit the concentration operation.

676. As established by the Merger Control Law, the merger test is aimed at determining whether a relevant concentration might cause a significant restriction to competition. Non-competition issues are not taken into consideration for this purpose.

677. The Merger Control Law does not provide for a specific list of conditions that might be imposed because of a merger control review. It is also important to consider that, given that the act entered into force in mid-June 2021, there is no relevant case law as to which take as a reference about the imposition of conditions to date.

678. Notwithstanding this, under the previous merger control regime, which was an enforceable force from 1997 to 2021 and applicable only to the electricity industry, there were three cases where the Commission imposed conditions for the approval of concentrations. These are:

(1) Edelnor (1998):[104] In a case involving the distribution company Edelnor (now ENEL Distribution Peru) the conditions imposed were intended to balance the companies' voting rights in the decision-making process of the Economic Operation Committee of the National Grid (COES) after the transaction, which oversees planning and managing the operation of the electric power generation and transmission system. COES' highest governing body is the Assembly, which is made up of the National Grid (SEIN) agents, grouped into four subcommittees, including generators, distributors, transmitters, and free users. The Commission considered that the new entity could gain decisive influence over its corresponding subcommittee because of the transaction.

    In this case, the Commission also imposed Edelnor (ENEL Distribution Peru) the obligation to bid for its energy acquisition among all the existing generators, to avoid any preference to its related generators (Edegel, Etevensa and Eepsa).

(2) Consorcio Transmantaro (2006):[105] In another case the Commission imposed a remedy by prohibiting the transmission companies controlled by ISA to participate in the second call for bidding for BOOT Contracts for Guaranteed Transmission Network Systems, to ensure that they present their best offer in the first call for bidding.

104. Resolution No. 012-1999/CLC-INDECOPI available in Spanish at: https://bit.ly/3dwWEkB.
105. Resolution No. 081-2006/CLC-INDECOPI available in Spanish at: https://bit.ly/3y7k7kk.

(3) Luz del Sur (2020):[106] In a recent decision, dated April 10, 2020, INDECOPI cleared a major transaction within the distribution and power generation segments (China Yangtze Power Co, a subsidiary of China Three Gorges Corporation acquired Luz del Sur). As part of its decision, INDECOPI imposed the condition that Luz del Sur should bid for its energy acquisition among all the existing generators to avoid any preference to its related generators. The bid shall be co-ordinated either by the electricity regulator, OSINERGMIN, or through a competitive and transparent process that shall be informed to INDECOPI. This condition intents to assure competition among generation power companies for serving the regulated market.

B. Timing

679. Under the Merger Control Law, the approximate term of the review procedure is a hundred and ninety working days at the Commission level (first instance), and a hundred and fifteen working days on appeal. The Commission's decision must be reached within Phase II of the review procedure.

§4. Relations with Other Merger Control Authorities

I. Other Authorities' Collaboration Within the Local Jurisdiction

680. Concentrations within the finance, insurance and pension funds sectors proceed with authorization both from INDECOPI and the financial regulator, the Banking and Insurance Superintendency (SBS). In case of imminent financial risk, only prior SBS authorization is required.

681. For concentrations involving agents active within the securities market under the surveillance of the Securities Market Regulator (SMV) requesting parties must obtain prior authorization from INDECOPI and the SMV.

682. Both the Commission and the Tribunal can request non-binding technical reports to sector regulators, such as OSINERGMIN, OSIPTEL, OSITRAN and SUNASS.

683. Finally, in the cases of procedures for the promotion of private investment through Public-Private Partnerships, the Peruvian Agency for Promotion of Investments (PROINVERSION) can request INDECOPI to issue a report on the possible effects on competition derived from a concentration resulting from the promotion procedure.

---

106. Resolution No. 007-2020/CLC-INDECOPI available in Spanish at: https://bit.ly/3qCQx3t.

II. International Coordination

684. Related to competition matters, the Third Final Complementary Provision of Legislative Decree No. 1034 (Competition Law) establishes that the NDC may exchange information, including information deemed confidential, with the competition agencies of the countries that are parties to an international co-operation agreement. For that purpose, INDECOPI has subscribed many co-operation agreements with competition agencies, such as Chile, Mexico, France, and the U.S.A.

685. The agreements that INDECOPI has signed refer to co-operation in matters of promotion of competition and other matters of its specialty.

686. The new merger control law establishes that INDECOPI may sign memoranda of understanding or other inter-institutional agreements with other national or foreign entities to guarantee inter-institutional co-operation. However, no treaty relating to merger control has been applied in Peru yet.

Chapter 4. Challenging the Administrative Decision

§1. Competent Courts

687. INDECOPI's decisions may be challenged before the judiciary in limited circumstances. Parties can challenge the administrative process and request the judiciary to declare the nullity or inefficacy of the administrative act. They can also request judicial review based on a violation of their constitutional rights during the proceedings ("*amparo*"). Significantly, the judiciary has the power to review the case on the merits.

688. Court proceedings for challenging administrative decisions are long and inefficient. Due to lack of specialization and overload, courts have insufficient resources to handle complex antitrust litigations. Extensive litigation hinders the system of enforcement of antitrust laws.

689. It is important to say that INDECOPI's judgments are characterized as res judicata and will be executed when they are final. In case of judicial review or challenge of the decisions before the judiciary, enforcement of judgments is not suspended unless ordered by the court in an interim measure at the request of a party.

690. INDECOPI has the power to enforce its own decisions (Article 48 of the LRCA). INDECOPI is authorized to impose fines to execute its decisions, being either interim measures or final judgments. Notwithstanding, courts play a fundamental role in protecting the interests of individuals and firms where competition authorities are unable or unwilling to enforce the execution of judgments.

§2. Time Limits

691. Parties have three months after notification of the final administrative decision.

§3. Scope of Judicial Review

692. As stated above, administrative decisions issued by INDECOPI's Commission or Tribunal can be challenged in the judiciary (Superior Court). Courts are authorized to declare INDECOPI's decision null if they consider that said administrative decision lacks any of the elements to be considered as a valid act of the administration. Most arguments exposed by those challenging INDECOPI's decisions involve a lack of due administrative process or the decision itself being unlawful as it derives from an erroneous interpretation of the relevant law.

Selected Bibliography

Alejandro Falla y Mario Drago. "Unas son de cal y otras de arena. Aplicación de la Ley de Competencia durante el 2011." (*Ius et Veritas* Nº 44, Tarea Gráfica Educativa, Lima 2012).

Alfredo Bullard. *Derecho y Economía. El análisis económico de las instituciones legales*. (2nd ed., Palestra, Lima 2009).

César Higa y Francisco Sigüeñas. "Las negativas injustificadas a contratar: aplicación y límites de la legislación de defensa de la libre competencia." (*Revista de Derecho Administrativo* Nº 10, Tarea Asociación Gráfica Educativa, Lima 2011).

Eduardo Quintana. *Libre Competencia. Colección por el Vigésimo Aniversario del INDECOPI.* (INDECOPI, Lima 2013).

Gonzalo Ruiz. "La nueva Ley de Represión de Conductas Anticompetitivas: acotando la discrecionalidad de la autoridad de competencia." (*Revista de la Competencia y la Propiedad Intelectual* No. 13. INDECOPI, Lima 2011).

Jorge Basadre, *Historia de la República del Perú* (9th ed., El Comercio, Lima 2005).

Jorge Fernández-Baca. *Experiencias de Política Antimonopólica en El Perú.* (Universidad del Pacífico, Lima 2012).

Luis Diez Canseco y Enrique Pasquel. "Precios abusivos: una mirada a la luz del Derecho Comparado." (*Advocatus* Nº 10, Lima 2004).

Marcial Rubio, *El Sistema Jurídico—Introducción al Derecho* (9th ed., Lima 2007).

Martin Tanaka, *Democracia sin partidos Perú 2000-2005* (Instituto de Estudios Peruanos, Lima 2005).

Selected Bibliography

Index

The numbers here refer to paragraph numbers.

Index

www.ingramcontent.com/pod-product-compliance
Ingram Content Group UK Ltd.
Pitfield, Milton Keynes, MK11 3LW, UK
UKHW020145290926
15471UKWH00004B/708

9 789403 543901